THE EASTERN QUESTION
1774–1923

The Eastern Question 1774–1923

REVISED EDITION

A.L. MACFIE

LONGMAN
LONDON AND NEW YORK

Addison Wesley Longman Limited
Edinburgh Gate, Harlow,
Essex CM20 2JE, England
and Associated Companies throughout the world.

*Published in the United States of America
by Addison Wesley Longman Inc., New York*

First published 1989
Fourth impression 1994
Revised edition 1996

ISBN 0 582 29195 X

British Library Cataloguing in Publication Data

A catalogue record for this book is
available from the British Library

Library of Congress Cataloging-in-Publication Data

A catalog record for this book is
held by the Library of Congress

Set by 7 in 10/12 Sabon
Produced through Longman Malaysia, GPS

CONTENTS

EDITORIAL FOREWORD

Such is the pace of historical enquiry in the modern world that there is an ever-widening gap between the specialist article or monograph, incorporating the results of current research, and general surveys, which inevitably become out of date. *Seminar Studies in History* are designed to bridge this gap. The books are written by experts in their field who are not only familiar with the latest research but have often contributed to it. They are frequently revised, in order to take account of new information and interpretations. They provide a selection of documents to illustrate major themes and provoke discussion, and also a guide to further reading. Their aim is to clarify complex issues without over-simplifying them, and to stimulate readers into deepening their knowledge and understanding of major themes and topics.

Roger Lockyer

NOTE ON REFERENCING SYSTEM

Readers should note that numbers in square brackets [5] refer them to the corresponding entry in the Bibliography at the end of the book (specific page numbers are given in italics). A number in square brackets preceded by *Doc.* [*Doc.5*] refers readers to the corresponding item in the Documents section which follows the main text.

LIST OF MAPS

ACKNOWLEDGEMENTS

I would like to thank Professor Matthew Anderson, of the London School of Economics, and Professor Malcolm Yapp, of the School of Oriental and African Studies, for reading a draft of *The Eastern Question* and suggesting a number of improvements.

The publishers would like to thank the following for permission to reproduce copyright material: Professor Matthew Anderson for extracts from his book, *The Great Powers and the Near East 1774–1923*; Routledge Publishers for an extract from C.J. Lowe, *The Reluctant Imperialist: British Foreign Policy 1878–1902*; Macmillan Publishers for an extract from R. Clogg, *The Movement for Greek Independence*; (c) Wadsworth Publishing Company for extracts taken from *Diplomacy in the Near and Middle East* by J.C. Hurewitz, published by D. Van Nostrand.

Whilst every effort has been made to trace the owners of copyright material, in a few cases this has proved to be problematic and so we take this opportunity to offer our apologies to any copyright holders whose rights we may have unwittingly infringed.

PART ONE: INTRODUCTION

1 THE EASTERN QUESTION

For more than a century and a half, from the Russo-Turkish War of 1768–74 to the Treaty of Lausanne of 24 July 1923, the Eastern Question, the question of what should become of the Ottoman Empire, then in decline, played a significant, and even at times a dominant, part in shaping the relations of the Great Powers. In the eighteenth century it concerned mainly the conflicts generated by the expansion of Russia into the territories bordering the northern shores of the Black Sea. In the nineteenth century, following the French Revolutionary and Napoleonic Wars (1792–1815), in the course of which a French expeditionary force occupied Egypt, it concerned the attempts of the subject peoples and their rulers to secure some degree of autonomy or independence, and the efforts of the Great Powers either to contain the tensions thereby generated or to exploit them to their own advantage. Thus in the 1820s the Greeks rose in revolt, and succeeded in securing their independence, despite the initial opposition of the powers; and in the 1830s Mehmet Ali, the ruler of Egypt, endeavoured to secure not only greater autonomy for Egypt but also the possession of Syria and a part of Anatolia, an enterprise eventually frustrated by the powers, who intervened to secure the preservation of the *status quo*. In the 1850s a Franco-Russian dispute concerning the administration of the Holy Places led to the outbreak of the Crimean War (1853–56), in which Turkey and a coalition of western European powers opposed what they saw as a further extension of Russian power in the area; and in the 1870s peasant rebellions in Bosnia and Herzegovina led once again to war between Russia and Turkey, and to the threat of war between Russia and a coalition of western powers. Not that the western powers were themselves averse to taking advantage of Ottoman weakness: on the contrary, in 1830 France occupied Algeria, and in 1881 Tunisia; while in 1878 Britain acquired Cyprus, and in 1882 Egypt. Only in the present century was the issue finally resolved. In 1908 Austria-Hungary annexed Bosnia and Herzegovina. In 1911 Italy occupied Tripolitania; and in the Balkan

Wars (1912–13) Serbia, Bulgaria and Greece drove the Ottomans from the greater part of their remaining territories in Europe. Finally, in 1918–23, following the defeat of the Ottoman Empire in the First World War (1914–18), the victorious Entente powers, in particular Britain and France, established a series of successor states and governments in the Arab provinces, while in Anatolia a resurgent Turkish National Movement succeeded in expelling the powers and setting up a Turkish national state, with its capital in Ankara.

Even the briefest of surveys would suggest that historians of the Eastern Question have not always agreed on its precise character and chronology. An anonymous English author, writing in the *Edinburgh Review* 1850, who believed that the question had become 'fully constituted' only at the end of the Napoleonic Wars, concluded that it concerned merely the question of what should become of the Ottoman Empire, then 'ruinous and unwieldy'. M. A. Ubicini, who edited a collection of documents, entitled *La Question d'Orient devant l'Europe*, in 1854, evidently believed that it concerned only the dispute regarding the administration of the Holy Places, then becoming critical. Max Choublier, a French historian, who published *La Question d'Orient avant le Traité de Berlin* in 1899, and who believed that the question originated in the eighteenth century with the decline of the Ottoman Empire in the area of the Black Sea, pointed out that it involved many questions, including the possession of the remaining Ottoman territories in Europe, Asia Minor, Syria and Egypt, and a possible resurgence of 'Muslim fanaticism' in Asia and North Africa. Edouard Driault, who published *La Question d'Orient* in 1909, and who believed that the question arose as a result of the retreat of Islam in Europe and Asia, concluded that it was primarily concerned with the resurrection of the Christian Balkan states and the advance of Turkey's Christian neighbours: 'Gigantesque croisade, auprès de laquelle celles du moyen âge furent des jeux d'enfants'. J. A. Marriott, who published *The Eastern Question* in 1918, believed that it involved six specific factors: the part played by the Ottoman Turks in the history of Europe since their first crossing of the Hellespont in the fourteenth century; the position of the Balkan states, following the subsidence of the 'waters of the Ottoman flood'; the question of access to the Black Sea, and the related questions of Constantinople and the Straits; the position of Russia in Europe; the position of the Habsburg Empire; and the attitude of the European powers in general.

A British Foreign Office handbook, entitled *History of the Eastern*

Question, published in 1918, took a similar view, arguing that the question was concerned merely with events in the Balkans, in particular with the problems created by the rise of Balkan nationalism and the encroachment of Austria and Russia. Three possible origins of the question were suggested: at the moment of the first appearance of the Slav peoples in the Balkans in the sixth century AD; at the moment of the first appearance of the Turks in Macedonia in the fourteenth century; and at the moment when Ottoman decline was first made evident in the eighteenth century. With regard to the advance of Russia, the handbook remarks, the Treaty of Kutchuk-Kainardji of 1774 appeared to mark the opening of the new epoch. Jacques Ancel, in *Manuel Historique de la Question d'Orient*, published in Paris in 1923, concluded that the question was born out of the dislocation of the Ottoman Empire and the rivalry among the European powers which this entailed. The question first became clearly formulated, he suggested, towards the end of the eighteenth century when, following the French Revolution of 1789, ideas of liberty and equality spread rapidly throughout the Balkans, and when, following the Treaty of Jassy of 1782, Russia acquired possession of substantial territories on the northern shores of the Black Sea. P. E. Mosely, who believed that the question originated, or at least became critical, in the 1830s (as the title of his work, *Russian Diplomacy and the Opening of the Eastern Question in 1838 and 1839*, indicates) concluded that it was concerned mainly with two questions – the future of Egypt and the future of the Straits.

Among more recent historians, Matthew Anderson, who published *The Eastern Question* in 1960, concluded that the question was concerned primarily with the efforts of the Great Powers to come to grips with the consequences of Ottoman decline, first made evident in the Russo-Turkish War of 1768–74. D. G. Clayton, who published *Britain and the Eastern Question* in 1970, concluded that there were in fact many eastern questions, including the struggle between Austria and Russia for the control of the lower Danube and the Aegean coastline, a struggle which started in the eighteenth century; the struggle for the control of Constantinople and the straits; Britain's conflict with France in north Africa, in particular with regard to the control of the Nile valley and the Suez isthmus; the control of the Mediterranean sea routes to India, particularly in the period following the opening of the Suez Canal in 1869; racial and religious issues, of baffling complexity; and economic questions concerning trade and markets. Finally, Malcolm Yapp, whose book,

The Making of the Modern Near East, was published in 1987, in what must be seen as a radical departure from the traditional view, argues that the eastern question, in the nineteenth century at least, was concerned not with the decline of the Ottoman Empire but with its recovery. This recovery, he argues, which began in the reign of Selim III (1789–1807), played a significant part in stimulating 'national opposition'. This opposition in turn provoked the intervention of the Great Powers, who sought to persuade the Ottomans to provide, not better or more efficient government, but less. The problem of the eastern question, he concludes, should be seen not in terms of 'determination' and the 'impersonal forces of economics and nationalism', but in terms of 'accidental elements', in the 'choices of men, made in the turmoil of events with imperfect information and with all the weight of prejudice to which men are subject.' There was 'nothing inevitable about the way the Eastern Question developed and no historical ordinance which decreed that the Ottoman Empire should disappear'. As for the part played by the Great Powers in the affair, they were motivated primarily by the need to preserve prestige:

> Neither the protection of the routes of empire nor economic interest nor even the balance of power in Europe weighed, in the end, against prestige. In order that they might remain great, Great Powers demanded to be treated as great. Important developments should not take place without their consent even if that consent was given only as the result of military defeat. The integrity of the Ottoman empire was like a bank on which the Great Powers could draw to make up the balance of their prestige. When the bank was exhausted there was no longer an easy line of credit in the Near East; such was the fate of Austria and Russia in 1914. [122, *p.* 92]

Such a 'new view of the Eastern question' is not adopted in this study, which follows a more traditional approach, emphasising the long term interests of the Great Powers in the question, which appear to have remained remarkably stable throughout. Nevertheless, Yapp's approach is to be welcomed, for it is certain to promote renewed interest in the subject.

2 THE OTTOMAN EMPIRE AND THE GREAT POWERS IN THE EIGHTEENTH CENTURY

Following the foundation of an Ottoman State in north-western Anatolia in the first half of the fourteenth century, the Ottomans concentrated on acquiring possession of the remaining Byzantine territories in Anatolia and the Balkans. Only when Sultan Mehmet II, the conqueror of Constantinople, had completed these conquests in the second half of the fifteenth century did the Ottomans turn their attention eastwards to conquer the Arab lands, acquiring in the process the titles of Caliph (Protector of Islam) and Servitor of the Two Holy Sanctuaries (Mecca and Medina). At the height of their power, in the second quarter of the sixteenth century, their empire extended from the Indian Ocean to the gates of Vienna (which Suleiman the Magnificent besieged in 1529), and from the Crimea to the Barbary coast. As Suleiman himself declared in an inscription carved on the walls of the citadel of Bender in 1538:

> I am God's slave and sultan of this world. By the grace of God
> I am head of Muhammad's community. God's might and
> Muhammad's miracles are my companions. I am Suleyman, in
> whose name the *hutbe* is read in Mecca and Medina. In Baghdad
> I am the shah, in Byzantine realms the Caesar, and in Egypt the
> sultan; who sends fleets to the seas of Europe, the Maghrib and
> India. I am the sultan who took the crown and throne of
> Hungary and granted them to a humble slave. The voivoda Petru
> raised his head in revolt, but my horse's hoofs ground him into
> the dust, and I conquered the land of Moldavia [53, *p. 41*].

In the following century, however, not only did the Ottomans fail to expand further but their advance was checked on several fronts. In the north-west, following a long and exhausting war fought in the closing years of the sixteenth century, their forces were expelled from the greater part of Hungary, while in the east, following an equally exhausting war, their troops were expelled from Azerbaijan and the Caucasus. In the Mediterranean, Ottoman naval supremacy was undermined: in 1565 an Ottoman expeditionary force failed to take Malta, and in 1571 an Ottoman fleet was defeated in the Gulf of Lepanto. Effective control of the north African coast (Tripoli, Tunis and Algiers) was lost, while in the Black Sea marauding bands of Cossacks succeeded in raiding Sinope, and even the outskirts of Constantinople.

Nor was the structure of Ottoman power secure at home. For a complex variety of reasons – including a weakening of the authority of the Sultanate; the collapse of the *devshirme* (Christian slave levy) and *timar* (land holding) systems; inadequate tax revenue; over-population; loss of trade (in the second half of the sixteenth century the India trade was increasingly transferred to the Atlantic route); and widespread corruption – the heavily centralised system of government created by the early sultans came under increasing strain. So great did this strain become that in the closing years of the sixteenth century Ottoman authority in Anatolia all but collapsed, as armed bands of discontented soldiery, landless labourers and free-booters roamed the countryside, extorting money and goods from the people; while throughout the empire local chieftains, disaffected military commanders and provincial governors established more or less independent dynasties and regimes. As the English ambassador remarked in 1607, it appeared that the Ottoman Empire was 'in great decline, almost ruined' [53, *p. 51*].

The process of decline was not unremitting. In the second half of the seventeenth century, under the leadership of a series of reforming viziers, in particular Köprülü Mehmed Pasha (1656–61) and Köprülü Fazil Ahmed Pasha (1661–76), order was in part restored. Successful campaigns were fought in Transylvania, Poland and the Ukraine, though a second siege of Vienna failed in 1683. In the first half of the eighteenth century many fortresses, towns and territories previously lost to the empire were recovered, including the fortress of Azov on the Sea of Azov (1711), the Morea (1718), and Belgrade (1739).

Such occasional successes, however, proved insufficient to reverse the tide of Ottoman decline. In the Ukraine, the Russians continued their advance, and in the 1750s they constructed two great fortresses between Kiev and Ochakov, on the Black Sea. One of these, as the Sublime Porte (the Grand Vizier's palace and centre of Ottoman government) was quick to point out, was just thirty hours' marching time from the Turkish border, and the other a mere seventeen. In a war fought in 1768–74 the Russians inflicted a series of defeats on the Ottomans, in battles fought near the fortress of

Khotin on the Dnestr River (1769), and at Kartal on the Danube (1770), while an Ottoman fleet was all but annihilated in a battle fought before Chesme, in the Aegean (1770).

The prospect of Ottoman defeat in the war of 1768–74 at once raised the possibility of a joint Austro–Russian partition of the Ottoman Empire. In 1772, therefore, Prince von Kaunitz, the Austrian chancellor, submitted two schemes of partition to the Empress Maria Theresa. In the first, which may well have been inspired by a scheme put forward a year or so earlier by Chevalier Massin (a Piedmontese officer in the Russian navy who had connections at the Russian court), it was suggested that Austria might receive Serbia, Bosnia, Dalmatia, Macedonia, Albania and the Greek coast as far as the Morea, while Russia might gain the remaining Ottoman territories in Europe, including Constantinople and the Straits. In the second, it was suggested that a new kingdom might be created, ruled over by a king chosen by Catherine II of Russia, and incorporating Macedonia, Albania, Thrace and the Aegean Islands, with Constantinople as its capital; while Little Wallachia, Bosnia, Serbia, Turkish Dalmatia and Belgrade would fall to the Austrians, and the remaining Ottoman territories in Europe to the Russians. As for Crete, Cyprus and the Morea, these might be incorporated in yet another kingdom, ruled over by a king chosen by Maria Theresa [95].

In the end these proposals played no part in the final peace settlement. The Russians were distracted by unrest at home, for in 1773–75 there was a great peasant and Cossack rebellion, led by Emel'yan Pugachev, a Don Cossack; and they refrained from pressing home their advantage. Meanwhile, the Austrians, who feared that partition would merely promote conflict with Russia, remained content to support the maintenance of the *status quo*; though following the conclusion of peace they did occupy the Bukovina. As Kaunitz remarked at the time, it would be contrary to Austria's interest to permit any substantial weakening of the Ottoman Empire [95].

However, the Ottomans were not able to escape the consequences of their defeat in the war of 1768–74 entirely. In the Treaty of Kutchuk Kainardji (1774), which concluded the war, the Russians took possession of the Kuban and Terek areas of the Black Sea steppe, and a stretch of territory lying between the Rivers Bug and Dnieper, and also acquired the port of Azov on the Sea of Azov, together with the fortresses of Kerch and Yenikale at the entrance to that sea. They also secured rights of passage for their merchantmen through the Bosphorus and the Dardanelles, which had previously been closed to foreign shipping; recognition of the independence of the Khanate of the Crimea, whose incumbents had for centuries owed allegiance to the Ottomans; and the right to intercede on behalf of the Christian religion and its ministers [*Doc. 1*].

The Austrians entertained no doubts regarding the strategic significance of the gains made by the Russians in the Treaty of Kutchuk Kainardji. As Baron Thugut, the Austrian representative in the Ottoman capital, pointed out, a Russian fleet, sailing from Russian bases in the Black Sea, might now within a matter of hours land an army of 20,000 men before Constantinople, whilst Russian agents could instigate rebellion among the Sultan's Orthodox subjects in the Balkans: 'With the news of a successful landing, the sultan will have no choice but to leave his palace, flee deep into Asia, and abandon the throne of the Eastern Empire to his successful conqueror' [*95, p. 152*]. Or alternatively, as Kaunitz pointed out, a 'small but good army' might advance rapidly through the Balkans and expel the Ottomans from Europe [*95, p. 152*].

In the decades following the Treaty of Kutchuk Kainardji, the Russians lost no time in exploiting the advantageous position they had won. In 1778 they established a port and naval base at Kherson, between the Bug and the Dnieper, and undertook the construction of a Black Sea fleet. In 1783, following a series of incidents, in the course of which tribes supposedly loyal to the Sultan fought with others loyal to the Tsar, they annexed the Crimea, the Kuban and the Taman peninsula, and established a protectorate over the greater part of Georgia. And in 1792, following yet another Russo–Turkish war (during which, significantly, Britain and Prussia threatened to raise an alliance of western European powers opposed to Russian expansion in the area of the Black Sea), they acquired Ochakov, the fortress town commanding the estuary of the Bug [3].

During these years the Russians did not abandon the idea of partition. In 1782, in a personal letter to Joseph II of Austria, Catherine II – whose dream it was to restore a revived Byzantine Empire, no doubt under Russian protection – proposed that a new Greek empire, incorporating Bulgaria, Thrace and Macedonia, with its capital in Constantinople, should be established, ruled over by her grandson, the Grand Duke Constantine. At the same time a kingdom of Dacia would be set up, incorporating Moldavia, Wallachia and Bessarabia, ruled over by her confidant and lover, Prince Potemkin [95]. In the event, however, it was not from Russia that the next major threat to the integrity of the Ottoman Empire was to come, but from France. In 1798, determined to strike a blow at the British, with whom they were at war, the recently installed revolutionary government in Paris launched an expedition designed to secure French control of Egypt and, as a decree issued by the Directory put it at the time, to 'drive the English from all their possessions in the Orient' and to 'dry up' that source of their 'corrupting riches' [*Doc. 2*].

PART TWO: ANALYSIS

3 THE FRENCH REVOLUTIONARY AND NAPOLEONIC WARS, 1792–1815

The idea of a French occupation of Egypt did not originate with the Directory. As early as 1770 Saint Priest, the French representative in Constantinople, had suggested that in the event of a partition of the Ottoman Empire, France should acquire Egypt; and in 1777 Baron de Tott, Inspector-General of French commercial ports in the Levant, had visited Egypt in order to prepare plans for its conquest and the opening of a route to India by way of the Red Sea. Again, during the Russo-Turkish war of 1787–92, it was suggested on a number of occasions that France might occupy Egypt, together with Cyprus and Crete. In 1795, following the outbreak of war with Britain, a French agent called Dubois-Thainville had endeavoured to negotiate an agreement regarding rights of passage through Egypt with the Mamluk beys (grandees) who ruled the country. Had the agreement been concluded it would, as Charles Magalon, the French consul in Cairo, pointed out at the time, have enabled a French army, embarking at Toulon or Marseilles, to arrive in India in a mere sixty days, compared with the six months or so usually taken by the Cape route [47].

It is not surprising, therefore, that in April 1798 the French Directory – determined to strike a blow at the British, and unable for want of naval supremacy in the Channel to undertake an invasion of England – should have decided to authorise the despatch of an expedition. Nor is it surprising that in May Napoleon Bonaparte, the young and ambitious Corsican general chosen to command the expedition, should have embarked with a force of 35,000 men, accompanied by an impressive band of scholars, archaeologists, linguists and geographers, at Toulon. Yet the British and Ottomans, usually well-informed regarding such matters, appear to have had little or no inkling of the direction the expedition would take.

Once in Egypt, Bonaparte lost no time in securing control of the principal centres. On 2 July he bombarded and occupied Alexandria; and on 25 July, following the defeat of Mamluk forces at Shubrakhit and Imbaba (the so-called Battle of the Pyramids), he occupied Cairo. These successes, however, were quickly proved worthless, for the British, on hearing of the destination of the expedition, at once despatched a squadron, by way of the Cape, to cruise at the entrance to the Red Sea – it was believed at the time that the French might have assembled transports in Mauritius, ready for a move to Suez. At the same time a British fleet, under the command of Lord Nelson, was despatched to the Eastern Mediterranean. On 2 August this fleet, coming up with the French fleet anchored at Aboukir Bay, captured or sank the greater part of it. As a result Bonaparte found himself trapped in Egypt, unable to advance or retreat. Nor did he succeed in escaping the trap when he invaded Syria in February 1799 – in order no doubt to secure the land approaches to Egypt, and perhaps also bases for an invasion of India by way of the overland route. Although he quickly succeeded in conquering al-Arish, a Syrian frontier fort, and Jaffa, where 2,000 of the garrison were shot in cold blood, he failed to capture Acre, which was held by Ahmad al Jazzar, the Ottoman governor of Sidon, with the support of a small British contingent under the command of Sir Sidney Smith. Thus frustrated, towards the end of May he withdrew his forces from Syria; and on 22 August, having received news of events at home, where great opportunities for personal advancement were opening up, he secretly embarked for France, accompanied by only a small group of officers, leaving his successor, General Kléber, to negotiate the evacuation of the remainder of the French forces from Egypt. This Kléber lost no time in doing, and on 24 January 1800 he concluded with the Ottomans the Convention of al-Arish, providing for evacuation. In the event, however, for want of British agreement, the Convention proved abortive, and an evacuation did not finally take place until September 1801, by which time British and Ottoman forces, including a contingent from India, had arrived in Egypt and accepted the surrender of the French garrison [44].

The threat of French expansion in the Near and Middle East provoked a response not only from the British, who had an evident interest in blocking any French advance in the direction of India, but also from the Russians. In September 1798, concerned at possible French intervention in the Balkans, they despatched a squadron through the Straits to act in support of the Ottomans in the eastern Mediterranean; and in January 1799 they concluded an alliance with the Porte, guaranteeing the integrity of the Ottoman Empire. Moreover, in 1799 they assisted the Ottomans in securing the expulsion of French forces from the Ionian Islands, in particular

Corfu, which the French had recently annexed. In September 1805, following the breakdown of the Peace of Amiens (1802) and the conclusion of an Anglo–Russian alliance aimed at France, the Russians persuaded the Ottomans to sign a treaty providing for Russian co-operation in the defence of the Ottoman Empire, the temporary opening of the Straits to Russian warships, and a renewed Russian occupation of the Ionian Islands, which Russian forces had evacuated in 1801. Finally, in 1806, when French victories in Europe had greatly increased the influence of France at Constantinople, the Russians occupied the Principalities (Moldavia and Wallachia), thereby provoking war [3].

The French evacuation of Egypt did not by any means conclude the involvement of the British in the affairs of the Ottoman Empire in this period. In February 1807, in an attempt to force the Ottomans to make peace with Russia – an indispensable ally if the war against Napoleon were to be carried to a victorious conclusion – they despatched a fleet under the command of Admiral Duckworth through the Dardanelles to threaten Constantinople. This operation proved ineffective, as contrary winds and tides so delayed the expedition that the Ottomans were enabled, with French help, to fortify the city. Shortly thereafter, when the French appeared likely once again to acquire a predominant position in Egypt – where Mehmet, the commander of a contingent of Albanian troops, had seized power – the British sent a force to occupy Alexandria [3].

The interests of the Great Powers in these years were merely strategic. In 1799 Count Rostopchin, the Tsar's chief adviser on foreign affairs, suggested that, far from assisting the Ottomans in the defence of their empire, Russia should join with France and Austria in seeking its partition. In 1807, at Tilsit, Napoleon and Tsar Alexander I agreed that, in the event of the Ottomans failing to negotiate a satisfactory peace settlement with Russia, France and Russia should combine to deprive them of all their possessions in Europe [*Doc. 5*]. Russia might then acquire possession of Bessarabia, Moldavia, Wallachia and the northern part of Bulgaria; France would gain Albania, Thessaly (as far as the Gulf of Salonika), the Morea and Crete; and Austria parts of Bosnia and Serbia. A proposal put forward by Alexander that, in exchange for French possession of Egypt and Syria, Russia might acquire Constantinople and Rumelia (Macedonia and Thrace) was, however, indignantly rejected by Napoleon, who is said to have exclaimed: 'Constantinople! Constantinople! Never! for it is the empire of the world' [81, *p. 39*]. Finally, in 1808, at Erfurt, Champagny, the

French Foreign Minister, suggested that France might support a Russian annexation of the Principalities in return for Russian support for France in Spain [81].

Surprisingly, in view of the extent of Ottoman involvement in the French Revolutionary and Napoleonic Wars, and the numerous schemes of partition projected, the Ottoman Empire emerged from the struggle more or less unscathed. In June 1807, the British, now determined to reach an accommodation with the Porte, ordered a withdrawal from Alexandria just three months after their arrival, and in 1809 they concluded a treaty of peace with the Porte providing for the restoration of Britain's commercial position in the Ottoman Empire; the imposition of an upper limit of 3 per cent on duties on British exports to the empire; and the complete closure of the Straits to the warships of foreign powers in time of peace. The Russians, fearful of a French invasion of the motherland, were obliged by the Treaty of Bucharest of 1812 to agree to an evacuation of the Principalities. They did, however, secure possession of the greater part of Bessarabia, together with a degree of autonomy for Serbia, which had risen in revolt in 1804. Moreover, as the dangers of a break-up of the Ottoman Empire were made plain (for Britain, possible French control of the Near and Middle Eastern routes to India; and for Russia, possible French expansion in the Balkans and the area of the Straits), British and Russian statesmen were increasingly convinced of the validity of the principle, enunciated by amongst others Prince Czartoryski, the Russian Minister for Foreign Affairs, in 1804, that the integrity of the Ottoman Empire must if possible be preserved [*Doc. 4*]. Indeed, Tsar Alexander was so convinced of this that, following his accession, he declared: 'It is one of the fundamental principles of my political system to contribute in every way to preserve the Empire of Turkey, the weakness and bad internal administration of which constitute valuable guarantees of security' [37, *p.* 222].

4 THE GREEK WAR OF INDEPENDENCE, 1821–32

In the period following the Napoleonic Wars, the Great Powers sought to discourage rebellion both in Europe and the Ottoman Empire. When, therefore, in 1821 a rebellion broke out in the Balkans, they offered the rebels little if any support, and took steps to ensure that they would not achieve their declared objective of an independent state. Despite all their efforts, however, the Greek rebels in particular persevered, and succeeded after a long and bloody struggle in establishing a Greek state – the first of the genuinely independent successor states of the Ottoman Empire.

The rebellion of 1821 was planned and initiated by a secret society, the *Filike Eteria* (League of Friends) founded by a group of wealthy Greek merchants in Odessa in 1814, and it aimed at the liberation not merely of the Greeks but of all Balkan Christians. Taking advantage of the fact that the Ottomans were engaged in an attempt to suppress Ali Pasha of Janinna, an overmighty vassal, and hopeful that Russia would be compelled to intervene on their behalf, despite assertions to the contrary – in 1820 Count John Kapodistrias, Tsar Alexander's Foreign Minister, himself a Greek of Ionian descent, had informed representatives of the *Eteria* that on no account would his master countenance rebellion – in March 1821 the society despatched a force of some 4,500 men (including Serbs, Bulgars, Montenegrins, Moldavians and the so-called 'sacred battalion' of 700 Greek students), under the command of Alexander Ypsilantis, a general in the Russian army and son of a former *hospodar* (governor) of Wallachia, across the River Pruth into Moldavia. There it was hoped it would link up with the forces of Milosh Obrenovich, the Serbian leader, and Theodoro Vladimirescu, a Wallachian rebel, and spark off a wave of rebellion throughout the Balkans [*Doc. 6*].

In the Balkans in general the rebellion proved a disaster. Failing to gain the support of the other rebel leaders – he had Theodoro Vladimirescu executed for intriguing with the Turks – Ypsilantis first led his followers to defeat, in a battle fought at Dragatsani on the River Olte, and then fled with the remnants of his force into Austria, where he was at once incarcerated in a dungeon. Only in the Morea, amongst the traditionally independent Greek Orthodox *klefts* (brigands and outlaws), *kapi* (militia men employed by rich Greek landowners) and *armatoli* (militia men employed by the Turks), a number of whom had served in British and French units during the French Revolutionary and Napoleonic Wars, did the movement find ready support. There, in April, at the monastery of Aghia Lavra, Germanos, the Metropolitan Bishop of Patras, raised the standard of revolt; and there during the following months the rebellion spread.

Whereas the Serb revolt of 1804 had initially been directed not against the authority of the Sultan but against the despotism and corruption of Jannissary (Islamised slave-troop) units operating in the area, it is evident that the Greek rising was inspired from the beginning by ideas of national independence which were then popular in Europe. In the Russo-Turkish war of 1768–74 Catherine II had called on the Christian subjects of the Sultan in the Balkans to rise in revolt; and in the French Revolutionary and Napoleonic Wars French agents had propagated ideas of national independence throughout the area. Moreover, in the decades preceding the rising, a number of Greek intellectuals – in particular Adamantios Korais, a noted Greek scholar, and Rhigas Pheraios, a Hellenised Vlach – had sought to encourage a revival of classical Greek language and literature amongst the Greek peoples of the empire. However, it is doubtful how far these ideas influenced opinion amongst the isolated and illiterate brigands and militiamen of the Morea who carried on the struggle for independence after the defeat of Ypsilantis's forces [31].

Following the uprising, the Great Powers lost no time in expressing their disapproval. On 12 May Tsar Alexander, convinced that the rebellion posed a threat to the established order in Europe, persuaded his allies, Francis II of Austria and Frederick William III of Prussia, with whom he happened to be in conference at the time, to join him in issuing a strong condemnation; while the British and French, convinced that the Ottoman Empire alone would act as an effective barrier against Russian expansion in the Near and Middle East, communicated their expectations to the Porte that the rebellion would be quickly suppressed. Nor, during the following months, when news arrived of Greek and Turkish massacres, did their attitude change. But reports of the massacres, and of the execution of Gregorias, the Orthodox Patriarch of Constantinople, and several bishops, did persuade the Russians to despatch an ultimatum to the Porte, demanding adequate protection for the lives and property of the Sultan's Orthodox subjects, and threatening a withdrawal of ambassadors [17].

Amongst the peoples of Europe, on the other hand, support for the rebels was widespread. In Madrid, Stuttgart, Munich, Zurich, Genoa, Paris and London, Greek committees were formed, funds collected, loans raised and volunteers despatched, so that the rebellion, ill-co-ordinated and ineffective as it generally proved, was sustained, and Ottoman attempts at its suppression were frustrated.

Nor were the Ottomans more successful in their later attempts at suppression. Hindered by the need to fight simultaneous wars against the Greek rebels, the forces of Ali Pasha of Janinna, Druz rebels and the Persians, with whom they happened at the time to be at war, and by the need to keep substantial forces on the Russian frontier, they proved unable either to suppress the rebellion or to impose an effective naval blockade of the Morea. In 1824, therefore, they called on Mehmet Ali Pasha, the ruler of Egypt, for assistance, with the result that in February 1825 Ibrahim Pasha, Mehmet Ali's eldest son, having first re-established Ottoman control in Crete (for which he received the pashalik (province) of Crete), landed a powerful force at Methoni in the Morea. From there he commenced a vigorous campaign, aimed at the complete extinction of the Greek cause in the peninsula.

Throughout these years the Great Powers for the most part continued to pursue policies of non-intervention. At a congress of the Holy Alliance powers (Austria, Russia, and Prussia) held in Verona in August 1822, the Greek question was scarcely discussed, and a Greek deputation was turned away unheard. Nor was there any suggestion of active intervention in June 1824, when the representatives of the powers assembled in St Petersburg to consider a Russian proposal that the conflict might be resolved by the creation of three autonomous Greek principalities: eastern Greece (Thessaly, Boeotia and Attica); western Greece (Epiros, Etolia and Akarnania); and the Morea, in which, as in Moldavia and Wallachia, the Ottomans might retain the right to exact tribute and garrison fortresses [17].

Increasingly, however, the Russians lost patience with this approach. Their trade in the eastern Mediterranean had suffered severely, and they were in any case engaged at the time in a separate and parallel dispute with the Ottomans over the implementation of the Treaty of Bucharest of 1812 – and this was in many respects for the Russians a more important dispute, as it involved their interests in the Caucasus and the Principalities. On 17 March 1826 they despatched what amounted to an ultimatum to the Porte, threatening war if the questions in dispute were not quickly resolved. As a result the British, concerned to prevent a Russo-Turkish war, and the possible collapse of the Ottoman Empire that such a war might entail, were obliged to alter course. On 6 July 1827 they concluded the Treaty of London with the French and the Russians which provided not only for the creation of an autonomous, vassal state, but also for mediation and the imposition of an armistice. Should the Porte reject mediation, then the powers might at once take steps to establish contacts with the rebels. Should either party refuse an armistice, then they might take steps to separate the belligerents, but without engaging in hostilities themselves. Paradoxically, it was this threat which led in the end to allied military intervention, and not the Russian ultimatum of 17 March 1826, for on 7 October 1826 Sultan Mahmud II concluded the Convention of Akkerman with the Russians, conceding virtually all their demands regarding the Caucasus and the Principalities. On 20 October 1827 an allied fleet which had been despatched to the eastern Mediterranean to enforce an armistice on the Ottoman forces in the Morea came up with the Ottoman and Egyptian fleets at anchor in the port of Navarino, and, sailing provocatively into the harbour, despatched them to the bottom [120].

The destruction of the Ottoman and Egyptian fleets at Navarino effectively ended Mehmet Ali's participation in the war, and on 9 August 1828 he signed a convention with the allies providing for an evacuation of all Egyptian forces from the Morea. This proved a welcome relief for the Greek rebels. In April 1826 Missolonghi had fallen to the Turks, and in August Athens; and in May 1827 a Greek rebel force had suffered a disastrous defeat on the plain of Analatos, near Athens. For the western powers, on the other hand, the Ottoman defeat at Navarino threatened disaster. On 31 November 1827 Mahmud repudiated the Convention of Akkerman, and on 20 December he declared a *jihad* (holy war) against Russia. Within a matter of weeks the Straits were closed to foreign shipping, and within months Russian armies were advancing through the Balkans and the Caucasus. Despite fierce resistance, the Ottomans did not prove capable of withstanding the Russian assault in the campaigns which followed. On 27 June 1829 Erzerum, the great fortress town in eastern Anatolia, fell, and on 19 August Adrianople, the fortress town protecting the European approaches to

Constantinople. Finally, on 2 September the Ottomans were obliged to conclude an armistice; and on 14 September, they signed a treaty of peace at Adrianople.

In the later stages of the war, in particular, the prospect of a complete Ottoman collapse filled the leaders of the western powers with apprehension. As the Duke of Wellington (from January 1828 the British Prime Minister) remarked, Turkish power was now gone, and with it the 'tranquillity of the world' [17, *p. 274*]. Nor was there much hope that a stable system might be raised in its place [*Doc. 9*]. One possibility, considered by Wellington himself, was the recreation of a Greek empire, ruled over by a European monarch appointed by the powers. Another, suggested by Prince de Polignac, the French royalist minister, which would have involved an extensive redistribution of territory not only in the Near East but also in western Europe, was the creation of a Greek state, ruled over by the King of Holland, whose kingdom was to be partitioned. A third, proposed by Kapodistrias, who in April 1827 had been appointed President of Greece, was the creation of a confederation of Balkan states, including Greece, Macedonia, Epirus, Serbia and Dacia, with Constantinople as a free port [3].

Fortunately perhaps for the peace of Europe, the powers were not called upon to consider such fanciful schemes seriously. Following their victory in the war, the Russians concluded that they had more to gain from the preservation of the Ottoman Empire than from its destruction [*Doc. 7*]. In the Treaty of Adrianople they remained content to secure merely an extension of their frontier on the Danube; Ottoman recognition of Russia's annexation of Georgia and eastern Armenia; changes favourable to Russia in the administration of the Principalities; an extension of the privileges enjoyed by the Serbs; freedom of trade for the Tsar's subjects in the Ottoman Empire; and guarantees regarding the passage of Russian merchant ships through the Straits. They also obtained Ottoman recognition of an Anglo-Franco-Russian protocol, drawn up in London the previous March, making provision for the creation of an autonomous Greek state, ruled over by a hereditary prince, with frontiers somewhat to the south of a line joining the Gulf of Arta on the Adriatic and the Gulf of Volo on the Aegean [4].

The acceptance by the Ottomans of the London Protocol did not conclude the Greek question. In the following months the British and French, who had previously feared that a newly-created Greek state would fall under Russian control, now decided that, if a Greek state were to be created, they would prefer it to be both strong and independent. At a conference of the powers held in London in February 1830, they therefore persuaded the Russians to agree to the creation not of an autonomous, but of an independent state, with a frontier stretching from the Gulf of Arta to the Gulf of Volo, including the Cyclades. As for the appointment of a hereditary monarch, it was agreed that the throne should be offered to Leopold of Saxe-Coburg; and when Leopold rejected the offer, it was made instead, in February 1832, to Crown Prince Otto of Bavaria, who accepted it [119].

Greece was not the only territory to be lost to the Ottoman Empire in this period. In 1830, following a prolonged dispute regarding unpaid credits, the French government, determined to maintain the prestige of the monarchy, despatched an expedition to occupy Algiers, which was still nominally part of the Ottoman Empire. Thereby commenced a French conquest of the Maghrib that was to take the greater part of the remainder of the century to complete.

5 MEHMET ALI AND THE EGYPTIAN QUESTION, 1832–41

No sooner had the Great Powers settled the Greek question than yet another crisis in the affairs of the Ottoman Empire occurred, threatening its survival. In October 1831, Mehmet Ali, the ruler of Egypt, having already secured control of the Hedjaz (1813), the Yemen (1818), and the provinces of Nubia, Sennar and Kordofan, later known as the Egyptian Sudan (1822), despatched an army under the command of his eldest son, Ibrahim, into Syria, to secure control of the three Syrian pashaliks (provinces) of Acre, Damascus and Aleppo which were traditionally dependent on Egypt. During the following months Ibrahim not only successfully laid siege to Acre, but also occupied Damascus, Jerusalem and Aleppo, and defeated Ottoman armies sent against him at Homs, and in the Baylan Pass, between Antioch and Alexandretta. Nor did he stop there. When attempts to negotiate a settlement failed, he advanced into Anatolia, where on 27 December 1832 he defeated yet another Ottoman force, commanded on this occasion by Reshid Pasha, the Grand Vizier himself, at Konya.

For the Russians, in particular, the prospect of a complete Ottoman collapse, accompanied in all probability by a scramble for territory and a European war, was not at all welcome. In January 1833, therefore, in conjunction with the Austrians, they brought pressure to bear on Mehmet Ali to agree to a suspension of hostilities; and when shortly thereafter Ibrahim, in defiance it would seem of his father's advice, resumed his advance, pausing only at Kutahya, just two hundred and fifty kilometres from Constantinople, they despatched a naval squadron to the Bosphorus to assist in the defence of the Ottoman capital. Such assistance, however, proved insufficient to persuade the Ottoman Sultan Mahmud to stand firm. Following the receipt of an ultimatum from Mehmet Ali, demanding not only the Syrian pashaliks of Acre, Damascus and Aleppo, but also the district of Adana, he concluded the Convention of Kutahya (April–May 1833), granting the Egyptian ruler possession of the Syrian pashaliks and the district of Adana for life;

though with regard to the district of Adana the grant was to be disguised by the appointment of Ibrahim as *mohassel* (collector of taxes) [44].

For the British, as for the Russians, the prospect of an Ottoman collapse posed a serious threat. Not only might it provoke a Russian seizure of Constantinople and the Straits, and the permanent closure of the Straits to British warships which that would entail, but it might also result in the creation of a powerful Egyptian empire, embracing Syria, Mesopotamia, Arabia and parts of Anatolia, which would be capable, independently or in conjunction with the Russians or the French, of cutting Britain's communications with India by way of the Near and Middle East. In the early stages of the crisis, however, the British, preoccupied with events elsewhere, showed little inclination to become involved. In November–December 1832, when Ottoman emissaries visited London in search of support, they were turned away empty-handed; and in January 1833, when Prince Metternich, the Austrian Chancellor, suggested that Britain join with the other Great Powers in proposing a solution to the problem, his suggestion was ignored. Only towards the end, as the extent of the threatened collapse became evident, did British ministers bestir themselves. By then, however, it was too late. Not only had Mehmet Ali succeeded in imposing his will on the Ottomans, but the Russians, in reward for their support, had on 8 July 1833 secured from the Sultan the Treaty of Hunkiar Iskelesi, which committed Russia and the Ottoman Empire to render one another substantial aid and assistance in the event of an attack on either. In a secret and separate article, it also defined the aid and assistance that the Ottomans might render as the closure of the Straits to foreign warships [*Doc. 10*].

The French likewise proved slow to appreciate the seriousness of the situation. Having established close relations with Mehmet Ali, whose army had been trained and equipped by French officers, they showed little inclination to impose limits on his plans for expansion. Only when the consequences became evident – in the form of a Russian military presence in the area of the Straits – did they intervene. They then took resolute steps, both in Constantinople and Alexandria, to secure a negotiated settlement and a withdrawal of the Russian contingent; but like the British, they acted too late to radically affect the course of events.

For the Russians, the Treaty of Hunkiar Iskelesi promised significant advantages. It provided some assurance that in time of war, Turkey being neutral, the Straits would remain closed against the warships of an enemy. It also created the possibility that, as Count von Nesselrode, the Russian Foreign Minister, later put it, in the event of an Ottoman collapse, the Russians might again be 'on the ground the first and the strongest in the theatre of events, so as always to remain masters of the question'. [85, *p. 20*]. However, the treaty did not in fact, as many in Britain and France believed at the time, secure for Russia the right to pass warships through the Straits at will.

In order to remove doubts concerning the precise significance of the treaty, Nesselrode on 17 August informed his ambassadors, in a despatch intended for communication to the powers, that the secret article attached to the treaty did not impose any new burdensome condition on the Porte. It served merely to 'state the fact of the closure of the Dardanelles for the military flag of the foreign powers; a system which the Porte has maintained at all times and from which, indeed, it could not depart without injuring its most direct interests' [85, *p. 11*]. Confusion regarding the significance of the treaty was not just confined to the British and the French. In 1838, when Tsar Nicholas I and Prince Menshikov, the Minister of Marine, resolved to despatch a squadron of the Baltic fleet to the Black Sea by way of the Mediterranean and the Dardanelles, Nesselrode was obliged to point out that it would be neither 'legal' nor 'politic' to do so, as the closure of the Straits to foreign warships laid down in the treaty applied equally to Russia. Moreover, if the Russians were to secure a privileged position, the British and French would at once seek similar privileges, the granting of which would undermine Russia's predominant position in Constantinople and the security of her southern provinces [85].

Once awakened to the danger that Russia might secure what Lord Palmerston, the British Foreign Secretary at the time, described as a 'kind of protectorate over the Turkish empire', the British and French mounted a sustained campaign aimed at the destruction of the agreement [110, *p. 72*]. In August 1833, they issued a strong remonstrance, seeking to prevent the treaty's ratification; and when this failed, they each independently empowered their ambassadors in Constantinople to summon their Mediterranean fleets should a Russian threat to the Ottoman capital arise [110].

Metternich too feared the possible consequences of the treaty. As he angrily informed the French Ambassador in Vienna at the time: 'It would be better for the Empire of Austria to face the risk of a war of extermination rather than to see Russia aggrandised by a single village at the expense of the Turkish Empire' [85, *p. 25*]. So, at a meeting of Austrian and Russian heads of state, held at Münchengrätz in September 1833, he warned Tsar Nicholas I of the threat that he believed the treaty posed to the peace of Europe; and in a convention concluded at that meeting, he secured Russian assurances regarding the preservation of the Ottoman Empire. Should events lead to a collapse of the empire, however, then it was agreed that Austria and Russia would act in concert in establishing a new order in the Balkans [4]. In fact there was little likelihood that Russia would attempt an occupation of Constantinople and the Straits without first reaching agreement with Austria, for by mobilising her forces in Transylvania, Austria could at any moment threaten Russia's land communications with Constantinople, by way of the Principalities and Bulgaria, and these were deemed essential if a permanent occupation of the Ottoman capital were to be undertaken.

In the years following the conclusion of the Treaty of Hunkiar Iskelesi, the British and French in particular remained profoundly sceptical regarding Russian intentions. As their agents frequently reported, the Russians were busy assembling an army of 80,000 men in Kherson and Sevastopol, capable of embarking for Constantinople at a moment's notice, while on the borders of the Principalities special units, capable of making a dash through the Balkans and securing Russia's land communications with the Ottoman capital, were in training. Moreover, of equal if not greater significance for the British, in Circassia and the trans-Caucasian provinces the Russians were on the march, threatening Britain's growing commercial interests in the Levant – in 1838 the British concluded a commercial convention with the Ottomans securing virtual free trade throughout the area – and her position in India [91]. Surprisingly, however, in April 1839, when Mahmud provoked the so-called second Mehmet Ali crisis, by sending an army under the command of Hafiz Pasha, the commander of the Ottoman forces in Anatolia, to re-establish Ottoman sovereignty in the Syrian provinces, it was to be the French, and not the Russians, who were to find themselves isolated and at odds with the other Great Powers.

In the second Mehmet Ali crisis, as in the first, the Egyptians proved too strong for the Ottomans. In a battle fought at Nezib to the north-east of Aleppo on 24 June, Ibrahim Pasha routed Hafiz Pasha's forces; and in July Mehmet Ali secured the surrender – in effect the desertion – of the Ottoman fleet. Nor did fortune otherwise favour the Ottomans. On 29 June, a few days prior to the arrival of the news of the defeat at Nezib, Mahmud died, leaving

Abdul Medjid, an inexperienced boy of sixteen, to take over the reins of government.

On this occasion, however, unlike the previous one, the powers reacted to the prospect of an Ottoman collapse with great promptness. On 27 July, following hasty consultations, their ambassadors presented to the Porte a collective note advising that the Great Powers were in agreement regarding the 'Question of the East', and inviting it to take no independent action, but rather to await the 'effect of the interest' which the powers felt for it [4]. The Ottomans accepted this invitation with alacrity, insisting only that no settlement should cede Syria to Mehmet Ali. It quickly became evident, however, that the powers were by no means as united as they had appeared. The British, Austrians and Russians remained determined to sacrifice the Egyptian ruler's ambitions in Syria to the greater imperative of the survival of the Ottoman Empire. The Russians also welcomed the opportunity of isolating France, which Nicholas saw as a sponsor of subversion throughout Europe. The French, however, freed now from the threat of an Ottoman collapse and a possible Russian seizure of the Straits, saw no reason to impose punitive terms on their client [*Docs. 11* and *12*]. In September–October, therefore, when Palmerston and Brunnow, the Russian minister responsible, proposed that Mehmet Ali should be deprived of Syria completely, or alternatively that he should be permitted to retain merely the pashalik of Acre for life, but without the fortress of St John d'Acre, they rejected the proposals out of hand. They did the same with a later, more generous proposal, that Mehmet Ali should be permitted to retain those parts of Syria lying to the south of a line running from Beirut to Lake Tiberius. In the following months French opposition to a curtailment of Mehmet Ali's ambitions in Syria and southern Anatolia did not diminish. On the contrary, at one stage Adolphe Thiers, the French Prime Minister, even contemplated war; and in July 1840, when the other powers, their patience finally exhausted, met in London to draw up a Convention for the Pacification of the Levant, they were obliged to do so without the assistance of the French, who chose rather to advise Mehmet Ali to consolidate his position in Syria and to prepare for war.

The terms of the convention agreed in London, though demanding, were by no means severe. Mehmet Ali was to be offered the hereditary possession of Egypt, together with the administration of southern Syria for life, in return for his submission to the Sultan and the return of the Ottoman fleet. Should he fail to accept this offer within ten days, then he would be permitted to keep only Egypt; and should he in turn fail to accept these terms within a further ten days, then, as the text of the convention put it, the Sultan would be permitted to follow such 'ulterior course as his own interests, and the counsel of his Allies, may suggest to him' [4, p. 51]. Encouraged, however, by the evident disunity of the powers, and by mistaken perceptions of his own strength, Mehmet Ali chose defiance. During the following months, therefore, British and Austrian fleets imposed a strict blockade on Syria and the Lebanon, where rebellion had in any case already broken out, and on 11 September they bombarded Beirut. Moreover, on 10–11 October a combined force of British and Turkish troops, supported by Lebanese rebels, defeated an Egyptian army commanded by Ibrahim at Beit-Hannis; and on 3–4 November a British fleet bombarded and seized the fortress of St John d'Acre which, as Ibrahim no doubt recalled, it had taken Egyptian forces ten months to capture in 1833. Finally, on 27 November, following the appearance of a British fleet before Alexandria, Mehmet Ali was obliged to agree to an armistice promising the return of the Ottoman fleet and the evacuation of Syria in return for an assurance that he would be permitted to retain hereditary possession of Egypt [110].

In the negotiations leading up to the Convention for the Pacification of the Levant, Russia's willingness to allay British fears regarding the rights she had apparently acquired in the Treaty of Hunkiar Iskelesi proved vital to their success. From the start Brunnow made it clear that if a Russian fleet were sent to Constantinople, it would act not as the agent of Russia alone but of the European concert. Nor, he declared, would Russia seek to extend the Treaty of Hunkiar Iskelesi when it expired in 1841. Rather she would seek the conclusion of a new collective agreement, guaranteeing the closure of the Straits. A clause to this effect was incorporated in the convention; and on 13 July 1841, when the crisis was more or less at an end, Britain, Russia, Austria, Prussia, and France, now reconciled, concluded a Straits Convention, formally recognising the determination of the Sultan to conform to the 'ancient rule' of the Ottoman Empire, whereby in time of peace and in time of war, Turkey being neutral, the Straits would remain closed to foreign warships [4].

In the period immediately following the defeat of Mehmet Ali and the withdrawal of his forces from Syria, the Ottomans had little difficulty in re-establishing an effective administration in the pashaliks. In Lebanon, on the other hand, they failed completely. In the ensuing years, the communities inhabiting Lebanon, in particular the Maronites (Lebanese Christians in communion with Rome) and the Druzes (a heretical Muslim community), engaged in a prolonged struggle for power, culminating in massacre and war. In 1842 a quarrel between a Maronite and a Druz at Dayr al-Qamar led to hostilities in which a town was pillaged and burnt; and in 1845 hostilities again broke out. Finally, in 1860, taking advantage of divisions within the Maronite community, the Druzes, with Ottoman approval if not actual support, launched an attack on the Maronites, aimed at their extinction. As a result, the Great Powers, in particular France (the power principally concerned), felt obliged to intervene; and on 9 June 1861 they promulgated an Organic Regulation for Lebanon, which, as modified three years later, formed the constitution of the Lebanon until the First World War [*Doc. 19*].

6 THE CRIMEAN WAR, 1853–56

When, in 1850, Prince Louis Napoleon, the recently elected President of France, demanded a reassertion and enforcement of rights previously granted by the Ottomans to Latin Christians in the Capitulations of 1740, he sparked off a conflict that was to lead eventually to a war in which Russia, the self-proclaimed protector of Orthodox Christians in the Ottoman Empire, was to find herself confronted by a coalition of the western powers.

The rights in question, originally granted to French Catholics in the Levant in the Capitulations of 1535 and 1673, and reaffirmed and enlarged in the Capitulations of 1740, concerned mainly the custody and administration of the Holy Places. There, in recent years, not only had the Orthodox Christian community, now preponderant both in numbers and in wealth, secured similar rights and privileges recognised by the Sultan, but they had also undermined many of the rights of the French Catholics, securing in particular possession of the keys to the north and south gates of the Church of the Holy Sepulchre and of the grotto of the Holy Manger in Jerusalem. As a result, the French Catholics, determined to reassert their rights, had appealed to Louis Napoleon, and he, heavily dependent on the support of French Catholics at home, had instructed his ambassador to raise the question in Constantinople.

The precise steps which led from conflict to war appear in retrospect clear enough. In September 1851 Tsar Nicholas I, fearful lest a mixed French, Ottoman and Greek commission appointed by the Sultan to look into the question of the rights of Latin Christians would find in favour of the Latins, despatched a note to the Sultan insisting that no change in the existing regime be permitted. When the Ottomans continued to respond sympathetically to French appeals, he instructed Titov, his ambassador in Constantinople, to threaten to leave instantly, if any change were actually permitted. In response, the Marquis de Lavalette, the French Ambassador, threatened to despatch a warship and blockade the Dardanelles, if the issue were not at once resolved in France's favour. Thus threatened by both Russia and France, the Ottomans responded by endeavouring to placate both. On 9 February 1852, following the appointment of a new purely Ottoman commission, they informed the French that it was their intention to concede a majority of their demands, at the same time issuing a firman (imperial decree), secretly approved by Titov, assuring the Sultan's Orthodox subjects that on no account would any change in the *status quo* be permitted. These contradictory communications, which were initially received with delight by both parties – the Greeks declared the firman to be a 'Charter of their Liberties' – proved less than successful in resolving the dispute. In May 1852 Louis Napoleon, angry at what he saw as further Ottoman prevarication, despatched a war- ship through the Dardanelles in flagrant breach of the Straits Convention of 13 July 1841; and in July a French squadron appeared off Tripoli, supposedly to enforce the release of French deserters who had taken refuge there. In November Nicholas responded by promising the Ottomans support in the case of a French attack; and in December, in order as he put it to indicate to the Porte that he would not be 'trifled with', he ordered the mobilisation of two army corps in southern Russia. Also in December, in a move which considerably extended the scale and importance of the conflict, he claimed the right, supposedly granted in Article VII of the Treaty of Kutchuk Kainardji, to protect not only the Orthodox religion but also the Sultan's twelve million Orthodox subjects. In February 1853 he despatched a special mission, led by Count Menshikov, a professional soldier, to Constantinople [*Doc. 16*], charged with securing a secret convention guaranteeing the Tsar's right to act as protector of the Sultan's Orthodox subjects [110].

Menshikov's mission proved peculiarly unprofitable. Following his arrival, accompanied by the Chief of Staff of the Russian 5th Army and a high-ranking officer of the Black Sea fleet, he at once mounted a sustained offensive aimed at securing Ottoman agreement to the proposed secret convention. On 6 March he succeeded in securing the resignation of Fuad Pasha, the Turkish Foreign Minister, and his replacement by Rifaat Pasha, supposedly more sympathetic to the Russian cause; and on 22 March he produced a draft of the proposed convention. Moreover, on 5 May he delivered to the Porte an ultimatum declaring that if the convention were not concluded within five days he would leave the Ottoman capital forthwith. When the Ottomans rejected the ultimatum – acceptance of which would, as Menshikov himself remarked at the time, have secured for Russia a predominant position at Constantinople – he made good his threat and departed. As a result, on 27 May diplomatic relations between the two powers were broken off, and on 3 July Russian troops crossed the Pruth and entered the Principalities. Their intention, as Nesselrode put it at the time, was not to make war but to secure merely some 'material guarantee' that might be held until such time as the Ottomans had acceded to the Russian demands [81].

In undertaking this vigorous assertion of their rights, the Russians believed, with some justification, that they could count on British and Austrian support. In January 1853 Nicholas had engaged in a series of conversations with Sir George Hamilton Seymour, the British Minister in St Petersburg, in which he had sought the renewal of an understanding regarding the future of the Ottoman Empire, secretly arrived at with Sir Robert Peel, the British Prime Minister, and Lord Aberdeen, the Foreign Secretary, in May–June 1844 [*Docs. 14* and *15*]. On this occasion, as on the previous one, the British had proved conciliatory, agreeing that some recognition of the Tsar's right to act as protector of the Orthodox religion was warranted, and promising that in the event of an Ottoman collapse they would consult with the Russians first, before approaching any other power. They had, however, pointed out that an Ottoman collapse remained a remote possibility and that an agreement limited to Russia and Britain alone might do more to bring about a general war in the Near East than to prevent one. As for the Austrians, Nicholas had been led to believe that the Convention of Münchengrätz (which committed the Austrians to consult with the Russians in any dispute threatening the survival of the Ottoman Empire) remained effective; and that in any case he could count on Austrian backing in his dispute with the Porte, as he was himself at that very moment rendering Austria vigorous support in a dispute that had broken out with the Porte over an Ottoman attempt to re-establish the Sultan's authority in Montenegro [3].

Whatever the extent of British and Austrian support for Russia in the dispute – and until February 1853, at least, it was by no means insubstantial – it did not survive the sustained campaign of threats and intimidation mounted by Menshikov in Constantinople. On the contrary, as both powers became increasingly concerned at the apparent threat to the independence and integrity of the Ottoman Empire posed by the Russian demands, they each in turn took steps to indicate to the Russians that they would permit no further escalation of the conflict. On 30 May 1853 the British Cabinet empowered Lord Stratford de Redcliffe, the British Ambassador in

Constantinople, to summon the Mediterranean fleet, should he deem it necessary. On 24 July the Austrians, at the instigation of the British and the French – who had both in the meantime actually despatched fleets to Besika Bay, just outside the Dardanelles – convened a meeting of the representatives of the powers in Vienna to negotiate a settlement.

In the weeks immediately following the despatch of the British and French fleets and the convening of the Vienna conference, it appeared more than likely that the western powers would succeed in imposing some restraint on the Russians. The Tsar had little desire for war; and in Vienna the representatives of the powers – the Russian representative failed to attend for want of instructions – quickly drafted the so-called Vienna Note of 1 August, consisting of a series of compromise proposals, including Ottoman assurances regarding the execution of the clauses relating to the protection of the Christian religion contained in the Treaties of Kutchuk Kainardji (1774) and Adrianople (1829); a further assurance that no change in the existing position would be permitted without prior French and Russian consent; and an extension to the Orthodox community of privileges previously granted to other Christian sects. It seemed likely that the Russians would accept this note. In their deliberations, however, the representatives of the powers failed to take adequate account of Ottoman opinion. On 20 August, following demonstrations in Constantinople in favour of a firm policy, the Ottoman Grand Council – convinced perhaps that the despatch by Britain and France of fleets to Besika Bay betokened the support of those powers, and encouraged by the recent arrival of an Egyptian squadron commanded by Said Pasha, Mehmet Ali's fourth son – boldly rejected the note, which, they declared, they would accept only on condition that it were made clear that the privileges enjoyed by Orthodox Christians derived not from international treaties but from an independent exercise of the Sultan's sovereign will. This condition the Russians in turn rejected; and towards the end of October, following the despatch of an Ottoman ultimatum demanding the evacuation of the Principalities within fourteen days, Russia and the Ottoman Empire found themselves once again in a state of war [3].

Following the outbreak of war, the stance adopted by the British and the French became increasingly belligerent. On 7 December Lord Clarendon, the British Foreign Secretary, instructed Seymour to warn the Russians unofficially that if Russian troops crossed the Danube, British ships would be sent to intercept and return men and stores despatched to the front from the Black Sea ports. On 4 January 1854, following the annihilation of an Ottoman fleet in the harbour of Sinope, the British and French governments ordered their fleets, now stationed in the Sea of Marmora, to enter the Black Sea. On 1 February they informed the Russians that it was their intention to implement the threat previously conveyed unofficially by Seymour; and on 27 February they despatched to Tsar Nicholas an ultimatum demanding the evacuation of all Russian forces from the Principalities. Finally, on 28 March, having in the meantime concluded a treaty with the Ottomans, committing themselves to the defence of the Ottoman Empire, they declared war [*Doc. 17*].

The Austrians did not remain indifferent to the threat posed by the war to their interests in the Balkans. On the contrary, they were determined to secure a Russian evacuation of the Principalities and the maintenance of the *status quo* in the area. In January 1854, therefore, when the Russians invited them to adopt a policy of benevolent neutrality, they replied forthrightly that they would do so only on condition that the Russians would undertake neither to cross the Danube nor to seek territorial advantage at the end of the war. Moreover, on several occasions thereafter they seriously considered joining the British, the French and the Prussians in an alliance designed to attain these objectives. On 20 April they concluded a treaty with the Prussians, committing Austria and Prussia to co-operation in the event of an attack on either; to the enforcement of an eventual Russian evacuation of the Principalities; and to joint action in the event of a Russian advance on Constantinople. And that was not all. Once assured of Prussian support, the Austrians unilaterally presented the Russians with a demand on 3 June that they evacuate the Principalities – a demand which the Russians, to the consternation of the British and the French, accepted, on condition merely that the Principalities should remain closed against their enemies for the duration of the war.

The neutralisation of the Principalities – later secured, with Ottoman consent, by an Austrian occupation – effectively removed any possibility that Britain and France might strike at Russia in that area. In September, unable for want of Prussian and Swedish support to attack in the Baltic, they despatched an expedition, which was later joined by a Sardinian contingent, to the Crimea, with the objective of capturing the great naval fortress of Sevastopol and destroying Russian naval power in the Black Sea. It was therefore in the Crimea that the great battles of the war, which cost over half a million casualties, were fought – on the Alma (20

September 1854); before Sevastopol (the fortress was not finally captured until September 1855); at Balaklava (25 October 1854); and at Inkerman (5 November 1854). In reality, however, there was little likelihood that the strategy adopted by the Allies would prove effective. Russia could not be brought down by a campaign mounted in the Crimea; and expectations that Russia's commerce would suffer severely from the closure of her Black Sea ports proved unrealistic, as the Russians were enabled, by an agreement with the Prussians, to re-route much of their trade to the north. Nor, despite energetic efforts, did the Allies succeed in making further progress on the diplomatic front, though on 2 December they did succeed in concluding an alliance with the Austrians guaranteeing the defence of the Principalities. Only in December 1855, when the Austrians, with the support of Prussia and the Allied powers, presented the Russians with an ultimatum demanding Russian acceptance of a set of recently agreed peace terms, which included the neutralisation and demilitarisation of the Black Sea and the cession to Moldavia of southern Bessarabia – a principal Austrian objective – was the deadlock broken. Faced then with the prospect of fighting a war on two fronts, and fearful of the possibility of rebellion in Poland, Finland, Podolia and Volhynia, and peasant uprisings at home, the Russians were obliged to give way, signing preliminary peace terms on 1 February 1856, and a treaty of peace in Paris on 30 March [3].

The terms imposed on Russia in the Treaty of Paris of 30 March 1856 indicate all too clearly the true objectives of the western powers in the Crimean War, namely the preservation of the independence and integrity of the Ottoman Empire, and the containment of Russian power in the area. As regards the independence of the empire, it was agreed that this should be guaranteed and respected and that henceforth the Sublime Porte should be 'admitted to participate in the advantages of the public law and system (*concert*) of Europe'. The Sultan, for his part, undertook to communicate to the powers the text of a recent firman proclaiming religious equality throughout the empire, it being clearly understood, however, that the said communication would not in any way give the powers, either collectively or individually, the right to interfere either in the relations between the Sultan and his subjects, or in the internal administration of the empire. As for Serbia and the Principalities, these would henceforth enjoy the protection of the contracting powers; and the Principalities, whilst remaining nominally subject to Ottoman suzerainty, would be permitted to establish an 'independent and national' administration. As regards the containment of Russian power, this would be achieved by the demilitarisation of the Black Sea, where no naval dockyard, arsenal or flag of war would be permitted; and by the cession to Moldavia of the southern part of Bessarabia. Finally, a revised Straits Convention, confirming the closure of the Straits laid down in the Straits Convention of 13 July 1841, was to be attached to the treaty, and an international commission set up to clear the Danube of impediments [*Doc. 18*].

The western powers were not content merely with the assurances contained in the Treaty of Paris. On 15 April Britain, France and Austria, determined further to emphasise their interest in the survival of the Ottoman Empire, signed a short treaty guaranteeing 'jointly and severally' the independence of the Empire. Any infraction of the Treaty of Paris would, they declared, be considered a *casus belli* by the signatory powers [4].

7 THE EASTERN CRISIS, 1875–78

The advantages gained by the western powers in securing the demilitarisation and neutralisation of the Black Sea proved short-lived. In October 1870 the Russians, seizing a favourable opportunity created by the outbreak of the Franco-Prussian War, unilaterally repudiated the demilitarisation and neutralisation clauses of the Paris treaty. However, in January–March 1871, at a conference of the signatory powers, where Italy and Germany attended as the successors of Sardinia and Prussia, they were obliged to submit their action to the powers for ratification. Nor did the reciprocal guarantees regarding the independence and integrity of the Ottoman Empire long survive the test of time. In 1875 the exactions of Muslim landowners and the influence of nationalist and pan-Slavic ideas sparked off rebellions among the Christian peasantries of Bosnia and Herzegovina which neither Ottoman authority nor Great-Power mediation could contain, and the powers quickly found themselves once again involved in a major diplomatic crisis, threatening not only the independence and integrity of the Ottoman Empire but also the peace of Europe.

The exactions of the Muslim landowners and tax farmers, which sparked off the rebellion, were indeed extreme. The Christian *kmets* (tenants, but in effect serfs) were expected to pay rent of a quarter of their produce and an animal from their flock annually; to work without payment on their landlord's land; and, on occasion, to provide free food and accommodation for their landlord and his servants. At the same time they were expected to pay heavy tithes and excise duties on grain, tobacco, vegetables, fruit and hay, and other taxes on land, houses, animals and beehives, whilst every Christian male was required to pay thirty piastres a year as a poll-tax for exemption from military service. Moreover, the tenant could not find effective protection against the extortion of landlord and tax-farmer in the courts, for the administration of justice remained venal and corrupt, despite the endeavours of a series of reforming Grand Viziers, in particular Reshid Pasha, Ali Pasha and

Fuad Pasha. (On 18 February 1856 Ali Pasha and Fuad Pasha, building on foundations laid by Reshid Pasha in the 1830s and 1840s, had persuaded the Sultan, Abdul Medjid (1839–61), to promulgate a *Hatt-i Humayun* (Imperial Rescript) reaffirming the so-called *Hatt-i Sherif* of Gülhane of 3 November 1839, which had promised protection for the life, honour and property of the subject; the abolition of tax farming; fair and open trials for persons accused of crime; and equality before the law for persons of different religion. These reforms were known collectively as the *Tanzimat* or Reorganisation.) As the British consul had remarked some years earlier, in Bosnia and Herzegovina the provincial authorities, with rare exceptions, acted according to the 'inspirations of their own personal interest'. If effective reforms were not quickly implemented, he predicted, then the area might soon witness scenes 'similar to those which have lately terrified Europe in Syria' [81].

It should not be assumed, however, that the rebellion was purely economic in origin. In recent years nationalist ideas and ideologies propagated in the period of the French Revolutionary and Napoleonic Wars and in the Greek War of Independence had found fertile ground in the Balkans. In the 1850s and 1860s the Montenegrans had once again asserted their independence, as had the Serbs, who in the 1860s founded theological colleges in Bosnia and Herzegovina in order to propagate pan-Serb propaganda. In Croatia and Dalmatia nationalist societies seeking Yugoslav unity under the Habsburgs, had become active; and in 1859, in Moldavia and Wallachia, a vigorous national movement had succeeded in uniting the Principalities to form the new state of Romania. Likewise in Bulgaria, where a renaissance of nationalist culture was underway, nationalists had in 1870 secured the restoration of an autonomous Bulgarian church, freed from Greek control.

Meanwhile, throughout the Balkans pan-Slav propagandists – inspired and supported by pan-Slav societies founded in Moscow (1858), St Petersburg (1868), Kiev (1869) and Odessa (1870) – were busy propagating the view that the Slav peoples of Europe should be united under the leadership of Russia. As General Fadeev, a leading pan-Slav propagandist, put it, in his *Opinion on the Eastern Question* (1876):

> The liberated East of Europe, if it be liberated at all, will require: a durable bond of union, a common head with a common council, the transaction of international affairs and the military command in the hands of that head, the Tsar of Russia, the natural chief of

all the Slavs and Orthodox ... Every Russian, as well as every
Slav and every Orthodox Christian, should desire to see chiefly
the Russian reigning House cover the liberated soil of Eastern
Europe with its branches, under the supremacy and lead of the
Tsar of Russia, long recognised, in the expectation of the people,
as the direct heir of Constantine the Great [4, *p. 88*].

Even amongst the Ottomans such ideas were beginning to make
an impression. In 1868 a group of Ottoman exiles, living for the
most part in Paris and London, who described themselves initially as
jeunes Turcs, and later as Young Ottomans, published a journal,
entitled *Hürriyet* (Freedom), in which they argued that 'love of one's
country' was 'a part of the faith', and proposed the introduction of
an element of consultation and representation into the Ottoman
system of government. In 1871, following the death of Ali Pasha,
who had pursued a policy of repression, and the proclamation of an
amnesty, many of the Young Ottomans returned to Turkey, where
for a time they were successful in propagating their views. But a
combination of bad harvests and the reckless extravagance of Sultan
Abdul Aziz (1861–76) led to further unrest, and many of the young
Ottomans found themselves once again the victims of repression
[67].

Abdul Aziz's profligacy proved extremely damaging to the
Ottoman Empire. Throughout his reign he borrowed heavily on the
London and Paris money markets. As a result, on 6 October 1875,
unable to pay the interest owing, the Porte was obliged to suspend
payment on part of the debt; and on 20 December 1881, following
negotiations with representatives of the European bondholders, to
hand over the administration of the debt to a Council of the Public
Debt, controlled by and responsible to the bondholders.

The immediate reaction of the powers to the uprising in Bosnia
and Herzegovina was one of either hostility or indifference. Tsar
Alexander II, who despite the enthusiasm of many of his subjects for
the pan-Slav ideal, remained committed to the preservation of the
Ottoman Empire, warned the Serbian government against intervention in support of the rebels. Count Andrassy, the Austrian
Foreign Minister, fearful lest the creation of an independent Slav
state or states bordering on Austrian Dalmatia and Croatia undermine the stability of the Habsburg Empire, likewise discouraged
intervention, as did Benjamin Disraeli, the British Prime Minister,
who urged the Ottomans to crush the rebellion as quickly and
effectively as possible. As for Prince Otto von Bismarck, the German

Chancellor, he remained indifferent to events in the Balkans, concerned only that the powers of the *Dreikaiser-Bund* (the League of the Three Emperors) – Prussia, Austria and Russia – should remain on good terms; while the Duke de Decazes, the French Foreign Minister, expressed concern lest the extra expenditure required might undermine the ability of the Porte to pay interest on the Ottoman public debt [82].

As the revolt spread, however, it quickly became evident that intervention of some kind would be required if war between Austria and Russia, the powers principally concerned, were to be avoided. In December 1875, therefore, Andrassy, with the support of the Russian ambassador in Vienna, drew up a series of proposals for the reform of the rebellious provinces, including a grant of religious liberty; an end to tax farming; an amelioration of the conditions of life of the rural population; the appropriation of direct taxes raised in Bosnia and Herzegovina to local purposes; and the appointment of a mixed Christian-Muslim commission to supervise the proposed reforms. On 31 January 1876, with the support of the powers, he presented these proposals to the Porte. Nor did the powers abandon their initiative when the rebels, sceptical regarding both the willingness and the capacity of the Porte to implement the reform programme, rejected the proposals. On the contrary, following a meeting held under the auspices of Bismarck in Berlin, Andrassy and Prince Gorchakov, the Russian Foreign Minister, drew up the so-called Berlin Memorandum of 13 May, which proposed a two months' armistice; direct negotiations between the Porte and the rebels; and Great-Power supervision of the reform programme – the principal rebel demand. However, if the new initiative proved unsuccessful, then the powers of the *Dreikaiser-Bund* would – as Lord Odo Russell, the British Ambassador in Berlin, put it in a report to Lord Derby, the British Foreign Minister at the time – supplement diplomatic action with such 'efficacious measures' as might be required in the interest of the general peace [99].

Though the proposals contained in the Berlin Memorandum received the support of the French and the Italians, they failed to secure the support of the British. As Disraeli remarked at a Cabinet meeting held on 16 May, they had good reason to resent the fact that they had been excluded from the discussions concerning the contents of the memorandum; and in any case, as Derby pointed out to Shuvalov, the Russian Ambassador in London, far from improving the situation, the proposals contained in the memorandum might merely exacerbate it, by encouraging the rebels to expect Great-Power intervention. In the event the proposals were never presented. In May a rebellion broke out in Bulgaria, in part inspired by revolutionary committees in Bucharest and Giurgevo and by pan-Slavs in the Russian diplomatic service – in particular Count Ignatiev, the Russian Ambassador in Constantinople, and Kartsev and Yonin, the Russian Consuls in Belgrade and Ragusa; and in the course of it massacres of both Turks and Bulgars occurred on a considerable scale. As a result, on 30 June Prince Milan of Serbia, bending before popular pressure, declared war on Turkey, as did Montenegro shortly thereafter; while in Russia news of the massacres evoked a wave of sympathy and support for the Bulgarian people. Similarly in England news of the massacres aroused public indignation and pity, together with a sharp increase in opposition to the pro-Turkish policy of the government. In September, Gladstone, the Liberal leader, published *The Bulgarian Horrors and the Question of the East*, in which he urged the expulsion of the Ottomans from Europe. 'Let the Turks', he wrote, 'now carry away their abuses in the only possible manner, namely by carrying off themselves. Their Zaptiehs and their Mudirs, their Bimbashis and their Yuzbashis, their Kaimakams and their Pashas, one and all, bag and baggage, shall, I hope, clear out from the province they have desolated and profaned' [99, *p. 75*]. As for Lord Derby, the Conservative Foreign Secretary, he was reduced to observing that 'any renewal of such outrages would prove more disastrous to the Porte than the loss of a battle', and that any sympathy previously felt in Britain for Turkey had now been 'completely destroyed by the lamentable occurrences in Bulgaria' [99, *p. 62*]. The consequences of the rebellion were not confined to the Christian nations. In Constantinople they gave rise to demonstrations, which in turn led to the removal from office of Mahmud Nedim Pasha, the Grand Vizier, and on 30 May to the deposition of Sultan Abdul Aziz and his replacement by Murad V, who in turn was replaced by Abdul Hamid II, his half-brother, in August [99].

Faced with this dramatic escalation of the crisis, the powers of the *Dreikaiser-Bund* had little choice but to reconsider. On 8 July, at a meeting held at Reichstadt in Bohemia, Andrassy and Gorchakov agreed that, whilst they would not for the moment themselves engage in war, they would, in the event of the Ottomans proving victorious, take such steps as might be required to secure the integrity of Serbia, and possibly also the independence of Montenegro and a degree of autonomy for Bosnia and Herzegovina (the Austrian and Russian versions of the agreement differ on the precise details). Should the Ottomans be defeated, on the other hand, then the Habsburg Monarchy (in 1867 Austria and Hungary created the Dual Monarchy) might acquire possession of a part or all of Bosnia and Herzegovina; Russia southern Bessarabia; and Serbia Old Serbia and the Sanjak of Novibazar. In the event of a complete collapse of the Ottoman Empire, then Constantinople might be declared a free city, Bulgaria and Rumelia granted independence or autonomy, and Epirus and Thessaly annexed to Greece [*Doc. 20*]. Bismarck, more logically, proposed a radical partition of the Balkans, in which the Habsburg Monarchy would dominate the western Balkans and Russia the eastern, whilst Britain would be permitted to acquire Egypt and the Aegean Islands, and France Syria. At the same time all three approached the British, with a view to securing their co-operation in case of partition, or their support in case of war, while the British, for their part, took immediate steps to strengthen their Mediterranean fleet [3].

Meanwhile the powers were taking steps designed to bring the fighting to an end. Throughout the summer of 1876 they worked hard to persuade the belligerents to conclude an armistice; and in September they succeeded in bringing about a temporary suspension of hostilities. When this collapsed, however, and the Ottomans, following a series of victories, threatened Belgrade, the Russians, fearful of the consequences of a Serbian defeat, delivered an ultimatum to the Porte, threatening a withdrawal of ambassadors if an armistice were not concluded at once. Faced with this threat of war, the Ottomans quickly concluded that they must give way, and at the beginning of November signed an armistice [99].

Following the armistice, the powers lost no time in returning to the search for a negotiated settlement. Within a matter of days, they agreed to convene a conference, in order to draw up a programme of reform that might be presented to the Porte. This conference was eventually held in Constantinople in December, and the Russians, who wanted to reach agreement but were nonetheless determined to press for a settlement in line with their own desiderata, at once took the initiative. In a series of preliminary meetings held in the first weeks in December, Ignatiev, who represented Russia, proposed the creation of a large autonomous Bulgarian state extending well to the south of the Balkan mountains, with a considerable coastline on the Aegean, to be administered in the first instance by a supervisory commission and policed by a foreign (in effect a Russian) occupation force. Lord Salisbury, the British representative, opposed these proposals vigorously, as he was fearful of the consequences of so substantial an extension of Russian power in the Balkans. After further discussions it was agreed that the powers should propose to the Porte the creation of a smaller, autonomous Bulgarian state, divided longitudinally into two provinces, to be administered by a Christian governor and an international commission, and policed by a foreign, non-Russian gendarmerie. At the same time it was agreed that the powers should propose that Bosnia and Herzegovina be united in a single province, administered by a governor appointed by the Porte, with the approval of the powers; and that Serbia and Montenegro should be permitted some small territorial gains. When, however, the powers put these proposals to the Ottoman delegation, Safvet Pasha, the principal Ottoman spokesman, at once made it clear that the Porte intended to reject them. They would – as Midhat Pasha, the recently appointed Grand Vizier, had pointed out to Salisbury the previous day – almost certainly result in the dismemberment of the Ottoman Empire in Europe. Moreover, in order no doubt to impress representatives of the powers with the capacity of the empire to undertake its own reform, Safvet Pasha on the same day announced the promulgation of an Ottoman constitution, guaranteeing equal rights to all the Sultan's subjects. Nor did the Porte prove willing to accept a modified set of proposals, presented on 15 January 1877. As a result, on 20 January the conference broke up; and on 24 April the Russians, having first tried unsuccessfully to secure a collective coercion of the Turks, and also having taken the precaution of concluding, on 15 January, a military convention with the Habsburg Monarchy, guaranteeing Austrian neutrality in event of a Russo-Turkish conflict, declared war [99].

The terms of the Austro-Russian military convention of 15 January 1877, and of a political convention, dated 18 March, which accompanied it, confirmed the willingness of the Russians to accept a compromise settlement in the Balkans. In return for their benevolent neutrality in the war, the Austrians would be permitted to occupy Bosnia and Herzegovina at a moment of their own choosing. For the duration of the war Serbia, Montenegro and the Sanjak of Novibazar would be established as neutral zones, and Austrian forces would be excluded from Romania. In the ensuing peace settlement Russia would make no attempt to create a large Slavic state, but she would expect to recover southern Bessarabia [3].

Prior to the outbreak of war, British military experts estimated that it would take the Russians a mere twelve weeks to reach

Constantinople. In the event it took considerably longer. On the European front they failed to capture Plevna, a little-known fortress in Bulgaria; and in eastern Anatolia, though they captured Kars on 18 November, they failed to take Erzerum. Only in December, when the resistance at Plevna was overcome, did their forces in Europe make rapid progress. They then marched 650 kilometres through deep snow in fifty-one days, occupying Adrianople on 20 January 1878 and advancing rapidly thereafter to within sight of the Ottoman capital. As a result, on 31 January the Porte was obliged to conclude an armistice [82].

Throughout the war the British Cabinet remained divided between those who wished to initiate a vigorous response to the Russian threat to Constantinople and the Straits and those who wished, as far as possible, to avoid intervention. On 25 April 1877 Beaconsfield (in June 1876 Disraeli had been made Earl of Beaconsfield), the most determined exponent of a vigorous policy, persuaded the Cabinet to despatch the Mediterranean fleet to Besika Bay; and on 6 June he instructed Sir Henry Layard, the British Ambassador in Constantinople, to seek Ottoman permission for the passage of the fleet through the Dardanelles and a military occupation of the Gallipoli peninsula. Moreover, on 21 July he persuaded the Cabinet to authorise a strengthening of the Malta garrison, and on 13 August a review of the offensive potential of the Indian army. At the same time, approaches were made to the Austrians, with a view to co-ordinating resistance to Russian expansion in the Balkans. Meanwhile Derby, the chief exponent of a policy of non-intervention, endeavoured where possible to avoid any action which might provoke war; though he was obliged to warn the Russians that any action threatening essential British interests in Constantinople, the Straits, Egypt and the Persian Gulf would be treated as a *casus belli* [82].

The British approach to the Sultan regarding the passage of the Mediterranean fleet through the Dardanelles evoked a negative response. So too, after an initially favourable reaction, did the approach to the Austrians regarding an alliance. However, on 29 May Andrassy communicated a memorandum listing seven changes which Austria would not accept in a post-war Balkan settlement. These included the acquisition by Russia of territory on the south bank of the Danube; a Russian occupation of Constantinople and the Straits; the creation by Russia of a large Slavic state; and the exclusive protection by any one power of the Balkan Christians. Nevertheless, as Ottoman resistance collapsed in the last weeks of the war, Beaconsfield once again approached the Austrians, proposing an alliance. On 23 January 1878 he ordered the fleet to sail for Constantinople – an order which was rescinded when news of the conclusion of an armistice subsequently arrived. During the following weeks tension did not however decrease. As the Russians continued their advance, and as the English continued to assemble forces in the Mediterranean, preparatory to an occupation of either the Gallipoli peninsula or the eastern shores of the Dardanelles – on 13 February the British Mediterranean fleet actually sailed through the Straits and appeared before Constantinople – war continually threatened [82].

The preliminary terms imposed on the Ottomans in the armistice were for the most part dictated by the Russian high command, which had taken over control of the negotiations, and they proved severe. An autonomous and tributary Bulgarian state was to be established, along the lines originally proposed at the Constantinople conference; Romania, Serbia and Montenegro were to be given their independence and additional territory; and Bosnia and Herzegovina were to have autonomy. Moreover, the Ottomans were to be obliged to pay a large war indemnity, and to conclude a new Russo-Turkish agreement safeguarding Russia's interests with regard to the Straits. In the peace treaty signed at San Stefano on 3 March the Russians did not relent, for it provided that the proposed Bulgarian state, which would be occupied by Russian troops for two years and ruled over by an elected prince, would stretch as far as the Aegean; while Montenegro, which the pan-Slavs favoured as being more reliably Slav than Serbia, would acquire even more territory. Elsewhere, in Bosnia, Herzegovina, Crete, Epirus, Thessaly and Turkish Armenia, reforms were to be introduced. As for the war indemnity, this was to be substantially increased, though part would be offset against the acquisition by Russia of the Dobrudja – which the Russians intended to offer to Romania in exchange for Bessarabia – islands in the Danube delta, and territories in eastern Anatolia, including Kars, Ardahan, Batum and Bayezid [4].

Throughout these negotiations the Russians were left in no doubt regarding the attitude of the Austrians and the British. On 8 January 1878 Emperor Francis Joseph pointed out in a private letter to Tsar Alexander that he would oppose the creation of a greater Bulgaria and insist on compensation should Russia annex Bessarabia. On 14 January Derby instructed Lord Loftus, the British Ambassador in St Petersburg, to inform Gorchakov that any treaty between Russia and Turkey affecting the Treaties of Paris (1856) and London

(1871) must be a European treaty; and on several occasions Beaconsfield declared forthrightly that Britain would accept no treaty that placed Bulgaria and the mouth of the Danube under Russian control, that turned the Black Sea into a Russian lake, or that threatened British interests in India and the east. On 25 January, therefore, Gorchakov, who quickly recovered control of Russian foreign policy, fearful lest the western powers raise up a coalition against Russia – Beaconsfield was at the time endeavouring to raise up just such a coalition – assured both the Austrians and the British that those aspects of the peace settlement which were of European interest would be decided only with the agreement of the powers. In March he accepted an Austrian suggestion that a congress of the powers signatory to the treaties of 1856 and 1871 be convened in Berlin to scrutinise the proposed settlement [99].

The British were not prepared to await the outcome of the forthcoming congress before taking further action. On 4 June, determined to neutralise the effects of the Russian acquisitions in eastern Anatolia, and to secure base facilities closer to the expected theatre of operation [*Doc. 22*], they concluded the so-called Cyprus Convention with the Ottomans, after Layard had been instructed to threaten a total withdrawal of British support at the congress should the Sultan prove unco-operative. This gave Britain the right to occupy and administer Cyprus, in return for a promise of support for the Ottomans in the defence of their possessions in Asia, should the Russians retain Kars, Ardahan and Batum in the peace settlement, and attempt further aggression [37].

At the Congress, which eventually opened in Berlin on 13 June, the united opposition of Austria and Britain to the creation of a greater Bulgaria proved insurmountable for the Russians. Indeed, even before the Congress met, the Russians had been obliged to make substantial concessions [*Doc. 23*]. On 17 April, following talks between Andrassy and Ignatiev in Vienna, Gorchakov promised the Austrians a substantial diminution in the extent of the proposed Bulgarian state; and on 23 May, following lengthy discussions, Shuvalov informed Salisbury, who had succeeded Derby as British Foreign Secretary, that Russia would agree to the creation of a smaller Bulgaria with no outlet to the Aegean. Moreover, the principality would be divided by the Balkan Mountains into two parts: a northern part, enjoying more or less complete autonomy, and a southern part enjoying merely administrative autonomy. At the Congress itself it was further agreed that the Russians would end their occupation of Bulgaria within nine months of the exchange of ratifications of the treaty; that the Ottomans would be entitled to garrison the frontier between Bulgaria and eastern Rumelia (as the southern part became known); and that the consuls of the powers would have the right to assist the Russian Commissary in its administration of the new principality [80].

In other respects too the Russians were obliged to modify the terms of the Treaty of San Stefano. Whilst it was agreed that Serbia, Romania, and Montenegro would be declared independent, none was to receive the substantial territorial gains envisaged in the earlier treaty. In compensation for a Russian annexation of Bessarabia, Romania was to be given the Dobrudja and islands in the Danube delta, and Austria the right to occupy and administer Bosnia and Herzegovina and, if need be, the Sanjak of Novibazar. Finally, in the east, Russia, whilst retaining possession of Kars, Ardahan and Batum, was to restore Bayezid and the Alashkert valley to the Ottomans.

For the British the settlement arrived at in Berlin could be considered a success. No longer would the Russians be permitted to create a potentially powerful Slav state in the Balkans possessing important harbours in the Black Sea and the Aegean, and capable of threatening Constantinople and the Straits. As Salisbury noted in a report composed on 13 July, the day the treaty was signed, they had succeeded in pushing back the 'political outposts of Russian power' beyond the Balkans [1]. Nevertheless, as the British were well aware, Russia's success in securing bases in eastern Anatolia posed a serious threat to Britain's position in the Near and Middle East. In particular they feared that in the future the Russians might advance from their newly-acquired bases to secure control of an outlet on the Mediterranean or the Persian Gulf. As a precaution, therefore, and bearing in mind that only by way of the Straits could Britain's naval power be effectively brought to bear in a war with Russia, they insisted on attaching a protocol to the treaty, to the effect that Britain's obligations with regard to the Straits were limited merely to a commitment to respect the 'independent determination' of the Sultan. In the period following the conclusion of the treaty they took steps – mostly abortive – to assist the Turks in initiating a series of administrative and judicial reforms in eastern Anatolia, which it was hoped might prevent a further Russian advance in that area [4].

For the Austrians too the settlement arrived at in Berlin could be considered a success. Without firing a shot, they had succeeded in preventing a major expansion of Russian power and influence in the

Balkans. They had also secured the right, at once enforced, to occupy and administer Bosnia and Herzegovina, possession of which would, as Andrassy later remarked, enable Austria-Hungary to 'master' frontier risings in the area more effectively and to bring the western half of the peninsula more permanently under Habsburg influence. However, as Andrassy's opponents frequently pointed out at the time, the fact that they had been obliged not only to abandon the traditional Habsburg policy of supporting the preservation of the Ottoman Empire, but also to occupy territories inhabited by a million and a half hostile Slavs, could not but give cause for concern [99].

8 THE EASTERN QUESTION, 1878–1914

In the decades following the Congress of Berlin the Great Powers remained for the most part committed to the preservation of the Ottoman Empire. Thus in 1887, when Britain and Italy, later joined by Austria, concluded the so-called Mediterranean Agreements – the British wished to strengthen their position in the Mediterranean against France and Russia, while the Italians and the Austrians, at the instigation of their mentor, Bismarck, wished to strengthen the position of the Triple Alliance – they committed themselves to the maintenance of the *status quo* in the Mediterranean and the Black Sea. In 1894–96, when massacres of Armenians in the Ottoman Empire provoked a crisis, France and Russia agreed to avoid intervention if possible and to seek the preservation of the *status quo*, as did Austria and Russia the following year. Yet on several occasions one or other of the powers took steps which led to a further fragmentation of the empire. In 1881 France occupied Tunisia, which was still nominally part of the Ottoman Empire; in 1882 Britain occupied Egypt; in 1908 Austria-Hungary annexed Bosnia and Herzegovina; in 1911 Italy seized Tripolitania; and in the years preceding the First World War, the Balkan states, for want of Great-Power intervention, were enabled to deprive the Ottomans of the major part of their remaining possessions in Europe.

France's occupation of Tunisia came after almost forty years of French involvement in the area. In 1836, following the re-establishment of Ottoman control in Tripoli the previous year, the French government despatched a squadron to prevent the Ottomans attempting a similar operation in Tunis. In 1857, in conjunction with the British, they forced the ruler, Muhammad Bey, to introduce reforms favourable to European interests and to permit foreigners to purchase property. In 1869, when excessive borrowing led to bankruptcy, economic collapse and rebellion, they set up an International Financial Commission to reorganise Tunisia's finances; and in 1877 they had a reforming prime minister, Khayr al-Din, removed from office. Finally, in 1881, having defeated Italian opposition, and having received assurances of British support in return for French approval of Britain's occupation of Cyprus, they occupied Tunis and imposed a protectorate, thereby completing French control of a substantial part of the Maghrib.

In the second and third quarters of the nineteenth century European statesmen frequently predicted that Britain, whose interests in the area exceeded those of any other power, would eventually occupy Egypt [*Doc. 21*]. The British, on the other hand, committed by the Treaties of London (1840) and Paris (1856) to the preservation of the Ottoman Empire, protested almost as frequently that they had no such intention [*Doc. 24*]. In October 1876, Beaconsfield dismissed the idea as mere 'moonshine', and when, shortly thereafter, Bismarck suggested that Britain might occupy Egypt, the British Cabinet rejected the suggestion out of hand [99]. Despite such assertions to the contrary, however, in 1882 the British, impelled by the need to secure effective control of what in recent years had become the principal staging-post on the route to India, were driven willy-nilly into undertaking an occupation.

During the closing years of the eighteenth century and the early years of the nineteenth, both the British and the French had made frequent attempts to develop communications with India by way of Egypt and the Red Sea. Only in the second quarter of the nineteenth century, however, when the development of steam power and increased political stability enabled entrepreneurs, for the most part British, to overcome the obstacles posed by monsoon winds, marauding Arabs, disease and shortage of supplies, did they succeed. A period of rapid development then followed, in the course of which a permanent and regular system of communications was established for passengers and mail (1837); railway lines were laid from Alexandria to Cairo (1856) and from Cairo to Suez (1858); and finally the Suez Canal was built (1869).

The British government generally welcomed these developments. Indeed, in 1834 they co-operated with the East India Company in providing steam vessels for use in the Red Sea; and in 1857, during the Indian Mutiny, they despatched large numbers of troops to the subcontinent by way of the so-called 'overland' route – a journey which lasted about thirty-seven days, compared with the three months it normally took by way of the Cape. On the other hand, they remained profoundly sceptical about the advantages to be gained by the construction of a canal, fearing that it would open up what the Foreign Office referred to as a 'second Bosphorus', and lead to disputes threatening the integrity of the Ottoman Empire and the interests of Britain in the area [47]. Following the opening of the Suez Canal, however, and its remarkable success – in 1870 486 vessels, 75 per cent of which were of British registration, used the canal, and in 1871 756 vessels, again 75 per cent of which were of British registration – they responded rapidly to the new situation. In 1873, when a dispute over tolls threatened to bring about a closure of the canal, they brought pressure to bear on the Sultan to ensure that it would remain open; and in 1875, when the Khedive Ismail, in financial difficulties, sought to dispose of a substantial parcel of shares in the company, Disraeli snapped them up, fearful lest control of the company pass into enemy hands. Nor was that all. In the statement of British interests in the east, which Derby communicated to Gorchakov on 5 May 1877, he made it clear that any Russian threat to Egypt and the Suez Canal would be regarded by Britain as a *casus belli* [47].

The course of events which eventually gave rise to British intervention in Egypt originated in the effective bankruptcy of the Egyptian government, brought about by the profligacy of the Khedive Ismail (1863–79) who in a few short years accumulated debts of £100 million, mostly to European bond-holders. In May 1876, following pressure from the bond-holders, Ismail set up the *Caisse de la Dette Publique* to manage the debt, under the direction of four foreign controllers, British, French, Italian and Austrian. In October he established the so-called system of Dual Control, whereby two controllers-general, one British and one French, would supervise the revenue and expenditure of the government. Far from resolving the crisis, however, these appointments led merely to further intervention. In August 1878, following an international commission of inquiry, the British and French brought pressure to bear on Ismail to set up an international ministry, headed by Nubar Pasha, an Armenian, and including a British minister of finance and a French minister of public works; and in 1879, when Ismail organised opposition to the new ministry, they brought pressure to bear on the Sultan to secure his deposition. On 8 January 1882, following a successful *coup d'état* organised by a group of discontented army officers led by Arabi Pasha, an officer of native Egyptian extraction – the military élite in Egypt was traditionally of Turkish or Circassian descent – they despatched identical notes to the new Khedive Tewfik (1879–92) assuring him of their support and insisting that it was their intention to maintain the existing system of financial control. This intervention, not surprisingly, served merely to exacerbate nationalist and anti-European sentiment. Nor did the despatch of a joint Franco-British fleet to Alexandria succeed in re-establishing the authority of the Khedive. On the contrary, it provoked riots in Alexandria, in the course of which about forty Europeans were killed. On 3 July, therefore, following abortive attempts to persuade the Sultan to intervene, the British Cabinet instructed Admiral Seymour, commander of a British squadron in the eastern Mediterranean, to bombard the fortifications of the city. In August, when the French Chamber of Deputies had defeated a government attempt to raise funds for a joint Anglo-French expedition – the French were at the time obsessed with the Alsace-Lorraine question and the threat of war with Germany – the British despatched an expeditionary force commanded by General Wolseley, which landed near Alexandria, then occupied Ismailia, and on 13 September defeated an Egyptian army, commanded by Arabi Pasha, at Tel-el-Kebir [66].

The significant part which European financial interests played in the events leading up to the British occupation of Egypt gave rise in later years to accusations, such as those contained in Wilfred Scawen Blunt's *Secret History of the English Occupation of Egypt* (1907), that the British government was primarily motivated by a desire to protect the interest of European bond-holders in Egypt. This contention found little support among those closely involved at the time. As Sir Stafford Northcote, Chancellor of the Exchequer in the Conservative Government that served from 1874 to 1880, later pointed out, British interests remained throughout primarily strategic: to secure for Egypt a dependable administration which would both maintain Egyptian credit and independence, and safeguard Britain's route to India. 'Our policy', he declared, 'was not a policy for the benefit of a number of creditors or bond-holders, or whatever you call them, but it was a policy of an Imperial character, and with the minimum of interference to maintain the position of that important country, so important in the chain of our communications' [89]. Gladstone, who took over the reins of government in 1880, explained the occupation in even simpler terms: 'Apart from the Canal', he wrote privately to Lord Ripon, shortly after the victory at Tel-el-Kebir, 'we have no interest in Egypt itself which could warrant intervention' [89, *p. 179*].

Throughout the events leading up to the occupation, the British continued to protest that they had no intention of occupying Egypt permanently; and indeed in the following years they made several attempts to withdraw. Thus in November 1882 Lord Dufferin was sent to investigate the possibility of an immediate withdrawal; and from 1885 to 1887 Sir Henry Drummond Wolff spent many weary months in Constantinople, trying to negotiate an agreement with the Porte regarding evacuation. All such attempts foundered, however, on the inability of the British to establish an effective regime, capable of maintaining order, and on their failure to reach agreement regarding conditions of withdrawal with the other powers, in particular the French, who objected to British demands for rights of re-entry in case of a threat of invasion or internal disorder arising. As the years passed, therefore, and when no agreement was arrived at, the British occupation became increasingly established, particularly following the conquest of the Sudan, completed in 1898; and in 1914, when the entry of the Ottoman Empire into the First World War on the side of the Central Powers obliged the British to reconsider their position, they officially declared the occupation to be at an end, and proclaimed a protectorate [77].

Where Britain's occupation of Egypt was inspired by concern regarding the security of the route to India, Austria-Hungary's annexation of Bosnia and Herzegovina was inspired by the traditional Habsburg determination to maintain stability on the southern frontier of the empire. In June 1903 a bloody *coup d'état* in Serbia had brought a pro-Russian, Peter Karageorgevich, to the throne, and in July 1908 the so-called Young Turk Revolution had over-thrown the reactionary regime of Abdul Hamid. The Austrians, afraid that these events might disturb the *status quo*, decided that the time had come to clarify the ambiguous status of the occupied provinces. On 5 October 1908, therefore, Baron von Aehrenthal, the Austrian Foreign Minister, having first reached agreement with Alexander Isvolsky, the Russian Foreign Minister, in a secret meeting held at Buchlau, a hunting lodge in Moravia [*Doc. 26*], proclaimed the annexation. The effect, clearly unforeseen by Isvolsky at least, was dramatic. In Constantinople, where the announcement happened to coincide with a proclamation of independence, published by Ferdinand of Bulgaria, so great was the sense of outrage that many called for war, and a prolonged boycott of Austro-Hungarian goods was instituted. Similarly in Serbia, military measures were undertaken, and compensation was demanded; whilst in Russia Isvolsky, charged with exceeding his powers in seeking to hand over Slav territory to alien rule, was obliged to renege on the agreement made at Buchlau, and eventually to resign. Not that there was much the Russians could do to recover the position. Russia's friends in the Triple Entente – in August 1907 Britain, having previously concluded an agreement regarding colonial disputes with France, Russia's principal ally, had concluded a similar agreement with Russia herself, thereby completing the so-called Triple Entente – proved unwilling to back their ally in the Balkans, while the Germans despatched what Sir Arthur Nicolson, the British Ambassador in St Petersburg, referred to as a 'diplomatic ultimatum' of the most violent character, making it clear that Germany would support Austria-Hungary to the limit of her resources. In the end, therefore, Isvolsky, unable even to persuade the powers to consider the question at a conference, was obliged to drop the issue. As for the Ottomans, they eventually concluded an agreement with the Austrians, recognising the annexation in return for compensation of two and a half million Turkish pounds and the return of the Sanjak of Novibazar [57].

Italy's occupation of Tripolitania, on the other hand, was inspired mainly by demographic considerations. For centuries Venetians, Genoese, Neapolitans and Sicilians had founded communities elsewhere in the Mediterranean. In the closing years of the nineteenth century, therefore, when emigration reached alarming proportions, numerous schemes of imperial expansion were contemplated. In 1911, Giolitti, the Italian Prime Minister, having first secured the approval of Russia – the last of the Great Powers to give its consent – despatched a somewhat bogus ultimatum to the Porte, threatening action if the safety of Italians living in Tripoli and Cyrenaica was not secured, and ordered his forces to occupy Tripolitania [61].

Initially the expedition went well. The Italian forces occupied the coastal towns without difficulty; but in the interior they proved unable to overcome the stiff resistance mounted by Senussi Arab tribes, whose leaders proclaimed a *jihad*. Nor did the Italians prove more successful in persuading the Ottomans to admit defeat. In April and June 1912 attacks on the forts guarding the Dardanelles, which obliged the Porte to close the Straits for a time, failed to bring them to the conference table, and an occupation of Rhodes and the Dodecanese mounted about the same time fared no better. In the end, therefore, the Italians were reduced to engaging in lengthy negotiations with a variety of Ottoman delegations in Lausanne; and peace was not finally concluded until 15 October 1912, when the outbreak of war in the Balkans obliged the Ottomans to settle [61].

The occupation by Italy of Tripolitania, and the apparent Ottoman weakness which it revealed, convinced the Balkan states that they might attempt the final expulsion of the Ottomans from Europe. In October 1912, therefore, Serbia, Bulgaria, Greece and

Montenegro, having first concluded a complex web of alliances and understandings – the Serbo-Bulgarian treaty of 13 March 1912, the most important of these, provided for joint military action against the Ottomans and a partition of Macedonia, for the possession of which Greek, Serbian and Bulgarian irregulars had fought for more than a decade – declared war. They were not disappointed in their expectations. Within a matter of weeks Bulgarian armies defeated the Ottoman forces at Kirk-Kilisse and Lula-Burgas, as did a Serbian army at Kumanovo; and on 24 March 1913, following the breakdown of an armistice concluded on 3 December 1912, a combined Serbian and Bulgarian force captured the great fortress town of Adrianople. As a result, on 30 May 1913 the Ottomans were obliged to conclude a treaty of peace in London, conceding to the victorious Balkan states the cession of all Turkish territory west of a line stretching from Enos on the Aegean to Midia on the Black Sea, with the exception of Albania, whose fate was to be decided by the Great Powers. In the Second Balkan War, however, which broke out almost immediately among the victors, joined now by Romania, the Ottomans succeeded in recovering Adrianople [57].

During the initial stages of the First Balkan War the Great Powers remained for the most part committed to the preservation of the *status quo*. On the very eve of the war, they despatched a note to the Balkan states, warning them that they must take no action likely to disturb the peace, and informing them that no change in the *status quo* would be permitted. As the extent of the Ottoman collapse became evident, however, they had little choice but to abandon this stance; and in the ensuing confusion each power sought to secure its own interests as best it could. Thus the Austrians sought to ensure that in any peace settlement which might be concluded, Serbia would be prevented from acquiring additional territory or access to the sea. The Russians sought to prevent a Bulgarian occupation of Constantinople and the Straits, which they believed might threaten their interests in the area. The British were also concerned about the threat posed to Turkey's control of the Straits. And the Germans, increasingly convinced that war with Russia and France was imminent, endeavoured, for the most part unsuccessfully, to reconcile a defence of German interests in the Balkans with the need to support the Ottoman Empire, where in recent years they had built up a strong position.

German interest and involvement in the Ottoman Empire was by no means new. In the 1830s several Prussian officers, including Count von Moltke, who later rose to become a field marshal in the

German army, had advised and instructed the Ottoman army; and in 1882 a German military mission, commanded by General von der Goltz, was despatched, which in the following decades succeeded in winning substantial orders for the German armaments and munitions industries. In 1888 a German group obtained a concession for the construction of a railway from Izmit, on the Bosphorus, to Ankara – in the same year construction of a line linking Constantinople and central Europe was begun – and in 1899 and 1903, following visits by Kaiser William II to Constantinople, Damascus and Jerusalem, a German syndicate, led by the Deutsche Bank and the Anatolian Railway Company, obtained concessions for the construction of a major extension of the Izmit-Ankara line to Baghdad and Basra, by way of Adana, Aleppo and Mosul. Finally, in 1913, following the disastrous performance of the Ottoman army in the First Balkan War, the Germans despatched yet another military mission to Constantinople, commanded on this occasion by Lieutenant-General Liman von Sanders [24].

For the Russians the growth of German power and influence in the Ottoman Empire posed a serious threat. Not only would control of the Straits give Germany a stranglehold on Russia's Black Sea trade – in the recent war between Italy and the Ottoman Empire a brief closure of the Straits had done immense damage to Russia's export trade by way of the Straits – but control of the Ottoman army would also enable the Germans to extend the field of operations to the Caucasus. In the decades preceding the First World War, therefore, the Russians were at pains to restrict the construction of railways in both the Balkans and Anatolia; and in November 1913, when the Germans agreed to send the Liman von Sanders military mission to Turkey, they protested vigorously, insisting that on no account should von Sanders be placed in command of an Ottoman army corps in Constantinople or the area of the Straits. Moreover, in the years preceding the war, they embarked on a major programme of naval construction in the Black Sea, aimed at achieving naval supremacy there. At a conference of ministers and experts, held in St Petersburg on 21 February 1914, they considered the possibility of a rapid seizure of Constantinople and the Straits in the event of war, and agreed to prepare for such an eventuality; though they also agreed that as the outcome of a European war would be decided on the western front, the main effort should be made there [61].

For the British too, Germany's growing power and influence in the Ottoman Empire posed a threat. German control of the Straits in time of war would enable the Triple Alliance powers to exclude British warships from the Black Sea, while command of the Ottoman army would enable them to strike at Britain in Egypt, Mesopotamia and the Persian Gulf. Like the Russians, therefore, in the decades preceding the First World War the British for the most part opposed the construction of the Baghdad Railway; and following the opening of a substantial section of the railway in 1904, they took steps to support British enterprise in the area, which it was believed underpinned Britain's strategic position [61].

It should not be assumed, however, that in the years immediately preceding the First World War the Entente powers were unsuccessful in protecting their interests in the Ottoman Empire. In a secret agreement, concluded in August 1911, the Russians secured from the Germans assurances that they would respect Russia's interests in northern Persia and the Caucasus, in return for a suspension of Russian opposition to the construction of the Baghdad Railway; and in an agreement concluded in February 1914 the French secured similar assurances regarding their interests in northern Anatolia and Syria. Similarly, in a series of agreements, drawn up in July 1913–June 1914, the British obtained from the Ottomans and the Germans a promise that no extension of the Baghdad Railway from Basra to the Persian Gulf would be undertaken without prior British consent. As for the Liman von Sanders affair, the Russians won substantial concessions from the Germans in January 1914, including the appointment of General von Sanders as Inspector-General of the Ottoman Army, a rank independent of territorial command [61].

Such agreements, however, did little to relieve the acute state of tension then prevailing in Europe. The assassination of Archduke Franz Ferdinand, the heir to the Habsburg throne, in Sarajevo on 28 June 1914, sparked off a war between the Central Powers and the Triple Entente in July–August 1914. The Ottoman Empire did not escape involvement. On 2 August the Ottomans, hopeful no doubt of a rapid German victory, concluded a secret alliance with the Germans, promising support against Russia; and on 10 August they permitted the *Goeben* and *Breslau*, German warships fleeing from a British fleet in the Mediterranean, to enter the Straits, in clear breach of international law. Moreover, on 9 September, having ignored offers put forward by the Entente powers to guarantee the independence of the Ottoman Empire, provided 'the Turkish government binds itself to give a written pledge to fulfil, during the present war, all obligations arising from neutrality, and in every way to facilitate the uninterrupted and unhindered passage of merchant vessels through the Straits', they expelled a British naval mission which had been despatched to assist with the reform of the Ottoman navy. On 17 September they closed the Straits. Finally, on 28 October, they despatched a fleet under Admiral Souchon, the commander of the German Mediterranean squadron, to attack Russian ports and shipping in the Black Sea, thereby precipitating not only the entrance of the Ottoman Empire into the First World War but also its ultimate collapse and partition [49].

9 THE FIRST WORLD WAR, 1914–18

During the early stages of the First World War the belligerent powers concentrated their efforts on the French and Russian fronts in Europe, where it was believed that the decisive battles of the war would be fought. But following the entry of the Ottoman Empire into the war, the Germans encouraged the Turks to mount campaigns in the Caucasus and in the Sinai Desert, which were designed to distract enemy forces from the main fronts; and the British, concerned about the security of their position in the Persian Gulf, despatched a hastily-prepared expeditionary force to secure control of the Shatt al-Arab at the head of the Gulf. Moreover, in February 1915 the British and French, responding to a Russian request for action against Turkey, launched an assault on the Dardanelles, which was designed to knock Turkey out of the war, influence opinion in the Balkan states, and open the Black Sea route to Russia. As a result the Russians, fearful of the long-term consequences of an Anglo-French occupation of Constantinople and the Straits, laid immediate claim to the area, and in the so-called Constantinople Agreement of March 1915 secured Allied recognition of their claim. Nor was this the only agreement concluded by the Entente powers in the course of the war. During the following years the Allies (later joined by Italy) made a number of pacts including the MacMahon Agreement of July 1915–March 1916, the Sykes-Picot Agreement of 3 January 1916, and the Tripartite Agreement of 18 August 1917, which not only provided for the more or less complete partition of the Ottoman Empire, but also laid the foundations for a series of bitter controversies in the post-war period.

Though the campaigns mounted by the Turks in the Caucasus and in the Sinai Desert caused the Entente powers serious embarrassment at a critical moment in the war, both in the end proved unsuccessful. In the Caucasus, where the Ottoman Minister of War, Enver Pasha, himself assumed command, an offensive mounted in December 1914, in the depth of winter, ended in defeat; whilst in the Sinai Desert an assault on the British forces defending the Suez

Canal proved ineffective, though in this case the Turks did succeed in withdrawing their forces to defensive lines in southern Palestine. Only in Mesopotamia did the Turks achieve success. There in November 1915 they succeeded in checking the advance of the British expeditionary force before Baghdad; and in April 1916, following a long siege, they captured the British garrison defending Kut-el-Amara [97].

The Anglo-French assault on the Dardanelles, mounted in February 1915, arose in part as a consequence of the Turkish campaign in the Caucasus. On 21 January the Grand Duke Nicholas, commander of the Russian forces in the Caucasus, enquired of his western allies whether they would assist in relieving Turkish pressure in the Caucasus by bringing pressure to bear on the Ottoman Empire in one or other of its 'most vulnerable and sensitive' spots [74, *p. 53*]. During the following week the British and French, determined to respond positively, considered a number of possible actions; and on 28 January, despite earlier advice that, in view of the recent strengthening of the Turkish garrison in the area, the operation could no longer be considered feasible, they decided on a naval expedition to force the Dardanelles. On 19 February and 18 March, therefore, two major assaults were launched; and when these failed to reduce the defences, which had been considerably strengthened by the Germans in the first weeks of the war, a rapidly-assembled task force was despatched to occupy the Gallipoli Peninsula. As Lord Kitchener, the British Secretary of State for War, put it at the time: '... if the fleet could not get through the Straits unaided, then the army ought to see the business through. The effect of a defeat in the Orient would be very serious. There could be no going back' [74, *p. 59*]. Nor was the enterprise abandoned when the task force in turn became bogged down. On the contrary, further reinforcements were despatched. Only in December, following the entry of Bulgaria into the war on the side of the Central Powers, further German reinforcement of the Straits defences, and the failure of a last, desperate attempt to break through the Turkish lines, was the enterprise finally abandoned, and the expeditionary force, which in the closing stages of the campaign had suffered a wastage rate of 20 per cent a month, withdrawn [74].

In the note of 4 March 1915 which Sazonov, the Russian Foreign Minister, despatched to London and Paris after the first Allied assault on the Dardanelles, the Russians laid claim not only to Constantinople and the Straits, but also to southern Thrace, a number of islands in the Sea of Marmora, and Imbros and Tenedos at the entrance to the Dardanelles. Moreover, in conversations held the following day with the British and French ambassadors, they made it clear that any failure on the part of Britain and France to concede the Russian demands might result in the withdrawal of Russia from the war and the conclusion of a separate peace. Faced with this threat of Russian withdrawal, the British and French, despite serious concern regarding the long-term consequences of a Russian occupation of the Straits, concluded that there was little they could do. As Sir Edward Grey, the British Foreign Minister, pointed out when the question was discussed in Cabinet: '... the urgency of the question was to remove Russian suspicion as to our attitude ... It was therefore essential to the progress of the war that Russia should know where she stands, more especially as the occupation of Constantinople might be imminent' [74, *p. 58*]. So on 12 March Sir George Buchanan, the British Ambassador in St Petersburg, was instructed to convey to the Russian government Britain's consent to the Russian demands, subject to the qualification that the war be prosecuted to a victorious conclusion, and that Britain should achieve her own aims in the Near and Middle East. On 14 April the French followed suit. British desiderata would, it was made clear, include free passage of the Straits to merchant shipping; the establishment of Constantinople as a free port; continued Muslim possession of the Holy Places; and the acquisition by Britain of a neutral zone in Persia. French desiderata would include a French sphere of influence in Syria and Cilicia [*Doc. 27*].

The objectives of the Russians, in thus seeking the realisation of what Tsar Nicholas II, in a manifesto issued following the declaration of war, referred to as Russia's 'historic mission on the shores of the Black Sea' [74, *p. 50*], remained those that had inspired Russian foreign policy throughout the preceding century: effective control of the maritime route from the Mediterranean to the Black Sea; protection of the Russian economy against the damage which an unnecessary closure of the Straits might inflict, such as that which had occurred during the Turco-Italian war of 1911–12; and the realisation of the age-old dream of the Russian people that they might one day secure possession of Constantinople, the source and inspiration of their Orthodox faith and culture.

Russia's insistence on recognition of her claim to Constantinople and the Straits, and the agreement of March 1915 to which it gave rise, forced the British and French to reconsider their desiderata in the Near and Middle East. Whilst the French wished merely to secure possession of Syria and Cilicia, the British were less certain how much or how little they wished to obtain. Following a prolonged study of the question, they concluded that since Russia – strengthened, as she would be, by the possession of Constantinople, the Straits and part of Anatolia – might in the future pose an even greater threat to Britain's communications with India by way of the Middle East than heretofore, Britain should seek to construct a strategic line of defence, and perhaps also a railway, stretching from Basra in the east to Alexandretta or (in the event of that falling to France) Haifa in the west. It was believed that this line could be held against Russia; though it was doubtful that it could be held against both Russia and France, a possible combination that had caused considerable concern in the closing decades of the nineteenth century [74].

It remained to determine the precise political structure that might be established in the area in the event of an Allied victory in the war. An inter-departmental committee chaired by Sir Maurice de Bunsen, a Foreign Office expert, which considered the question in April–May, suggested four possible solutions. The first proposed the preservation of an Ottoman state in Anatolia, but the complete partition of the Arab provinces. The second proposed the preservation of the Ottoman Empire, nominally independent, but under effective European control. The third, the most conservative, proposed the preservation of the Ottoman Empire in Asia as an independent state, under the existing form of government. The fourth, which also provided for the preservation of the empire, proposed that it should be decentralised along federal lines. In their final report the committee, fearful of the conflicts which a more aggressive policy might inspire, opted for the fourth solution. In their study of the question, however, they paid particular attention to the advantages which would arise from partition. These, it was suggested, would include the preservation of Britain's interests in the vicinity of the Persian Gulf, generally agreed to be of overriding importance; greater freedom for Britain to restore, develop and exploit the wealth of Mesopotamia, a 'definite gain to mankind as a whole'; and the prevention of further Russian and German expansion in the area. 'Under a policy of partition', it was pointed out, 'British desiderata would be adequately met by the annexation of the vilayets [administrative units or provinces] of Basra, Baghdad, and the greater part of Mosul, with a port on the Eastern Mediterranean at Haifa, and British railway connections between this port and the Persian Gulf' [64, *p. 247*].

The need felt by the British to identify the nature and extent of their claims on the Ottoman estate was further exacerbated by a series of agreements concluded by Sir Henry MacMahon, the British High Commissioner in Egypt, with Sharif Husain of Mecca, in July 1915–March 1916, with the object of raising an Arab revolt in the Hedjaz and securing thereby access to Mecca and Medina for Muslim inhabitants of the British Empire wishing to go on pilgrimage. As early as September 1914 Kitchener had approached Husain, enquiring of him what attitude he would adopt in the event of an Ottoman entry into the war on the side of the Central Powers. In July 1915, by which time Husain had established contact with discontented Arab officers serving in Ottoman units in Syria and Iraq, further approaches were made; and on 24 October 1915 MacMahon despatched a note to Husain declaring that Britain would recognise and support the independence of the Arab peoples in Arabia and the Fertile Crescent, provided that the 'districts of Mersina and Alexandretta and portions of Syria lying to the west of the districts of Damascus, Homs, Hama and Aleppo' were excluded; that existing British treaty rights with Arab chiefs would remain in force; that the agreement would apply merely to regions wherein Britain was free to act 'without detriment to the interests of her ally, France'; and that special administrative arrangements would be made in the vilayets of Baghdad and Basra in order to secure established British interests there [4, p. 161].

The British were not at one in their view of the advantages to be gained from the promotion of an Arab revolt. The Government of India, in particular, remained sceptical. As the Viceroy, Lord Hardinge, pointed out at the time, Britain had traditionally regarded the creation of a strong Arab state lying astride her communications with India as a likely source of future trouble; while Austen Chamberlain, the Secretary of State for India, who described Husain as a 'nonentity without power to carry out his proposals', doubted whether the Arabs were capable of unity [30, p. 93].

The British declaration of 24 October did not conclude the debate. During the following months Husain continued to press for further assurances of British support, and to insist that Aleppo and Beirut, and even the whole of Syria, must be included in the proposed independent Arab kingdom. Nevertheless, it proved sufficient to convince Husain that he might safely raise the standard of revolt in the Hedjaz. On 10 June 1916 he occupied Mecca. During the following months, with the support and assistance of a small group of British officers, including Colonel T. E. Lawrence (later to acquire fame as Lawrence of Arabia), he launched a series of attacks on Ottoman forces and installations, in particular the Hedjaz railway, which caused the Ottomans considerable discomfort [97].

On 3 January 1916, in order further to define and delimit the territories in which Britain and France might be expected to exercise direct and indirect control and influence in the Ottoman Empire following its defeat and partition, and by implication the territories in which the Arabs might be permitted to establish an Arab state or confederation of states, the British and French concluded the Sykes-Picot Agreement, named after Sir Mark Sykes, Assistant Secretary to the British War Cabinet, and Charles Picot, a French diplomat, who negotiated it. According to the terms of this agreement it was established that, in the Baghdad–Basra region of lower Iraq, Britain might exercise direct control and in Cilicia and the northern Syrian litoral, France. In the remainder of the Fertile Crescent and the Syrian interior, Britain might exercise indirect control in the south and France in the north. Britain would in addition obtain control of a small enclave on the Palestinian coast, including Haifa and Acre (suitable for a rail terminal), whilst the rest of Palestine would be placed under an international administration [4]. The Russians and the Italians were also included in the agreement. In March 1916, following a visit by Sykes and Picot to St Petersburg, it was agreed that, in return for Russian recognition of the Sykes–Picot agreement, Russia might be permitted to acquire the vilayets of Van, Bitlis, Trebizond and Erzerum, where in the first year or so of the war more than three-quarters of a million Armenians had suffered deportation and massacre as a result of measures supposedly implemented by the Ottomans to secure the defence of the eastern frontier. In August 1917, following Italy's entry into the war on the side of the Allies, it was agreed in the Tripartite Agreement negotiated at St Jean de Maurienne that, subject to Russian consent, Italy might acquire a sphere of influence in western Anatolia, including Smyrna (already informally promised to the Greeks), Antalya and Aidin [3].

The Sykes-Picot and Tripartite agreements were by no means the final statement of Allied intentions in the First World War. In the remaining months of the war the British and the Americans in particular issued a number of contradictory declarations, further compounding the contradictions inherent in the earlier agreements. On 2 November 1917, in a desperate bid to secure the support of Russian and American Jewry for the Allied war effort, Lord Balfour, the British Foreign Secretary, issued the so-called Balfour Declaration, promising British support for the establishment in Palestine of a 'National Home' for the Jewish people, 'it being clearly understood that nothing shall be done which may prejudice the civil and religious rights of the existing non-Jewish communities' [*Doc. 28*]. On 8 January 1918 President Woodrow Wilson published a list of peace terms, later known as the Fourteen Points, proposing an end to secret agreements and autonomy for the subject peoples of the Ottoman Empire [*Doc. 29*]. Finally, on 16 June 1918, in a public declaration, later known as the Declaration to the Seven, issued in response to enquiries from a group of eminent Syrians resident in Egypt, the British stated that with regard to areas in Arabia which had been free and independent before the outbreak of war, and areas emancipated by the actions of the Arabs themselves, Britain would recognise the 'complete and sovereign independence of the Arab peoples' [44, *p. 276*]. In areas liberated by the actions of Allied armies, on the other hand, British policy was that future government should be based on the principle of the consent of the governed. As for territories which might remain under Turkish control, it was to be hoped that the inhabitants of these would quickly secure their freedom and independence [44].

In 1917 the Allied forces in Arabia and the Fertile Crescent increasingly gained the upper hand. In March the British expeditionary force in Iraq at long last succeeded in occupying Baghdad. In July Husain's irregular forces in Arabia, under the command of Emir Faisal, Husain's third son, captured Aqaba, at the head of the Gulf of Aqaba, and advanced to link up with the British expeditionary force commanded by General Allenby, which was advancing into Palestine. In October–December Allenby himself broke through the Turkish lines and captured Jerusalem, though stiff Turkish resistance prevented further advances until the closing weeks of the war [83].

In Russia, on the other hand, the Allies suffered a series of reverses. During the summer of 1917 confidence in the provisional government which had been appointed in March after the abdication of the Tsar, collapsed; and in October the Bolsheviks seized power. In December they opened peace negotiations with the Germans, and on 3 March 1918 concluded the Treaty of Brest-Litovsk, which ended the war in the east. Moreover, in the Decree of Peace of 8 November 1917 and the Appeal to the Muslim Workers of Russia and the East of 7 December, they denounced both Russia's war aims and the secret treaties that embodied them, in particular those concerning Constantinople, the Straits and the Armenian provinces. Such reverses, however, proved insufficient to save the Ottoman Empire. On 31 October, following defeats on the Syrian front and the surrender of Bulgaria, the Ottomans were obliged to conclude an armistice with the Allies, agreeing to a complete suspension of hostilities, the immediate demobilisation of the Ottoman armed forces and the occupation of any part of Turkey deemed necessary to Allied security. During the negotiation of the armistice, Raouf Bey, the leader of the Ottoman delegation, insisted that on no account should Greek and Italian forces be permitted to share in the occupation. If they were, he predicted, it would almost certainly mean 'revolution in the country' [74, *p. 68*].

10 THE PEACE SETTLEMENT, 1918–23

Following their victory in the First World War, the western Entente powers turned their attention to the task of establishing a new order in the Near and Middle East. This was based for the most part not on the principle of self-determination embodied in the Fourteen Points, but on the principle of partition enshrined in the secret treaties and agreements which remained effective – with the exception of the Constantinople Agreement of March 1915 and the Tripartite Agreement of August 1917 (the Constantinople Agreement had lapsed on the withdrawal of Russia from the war, and the Tripartite Agreement had been made subject to Russian consent, never obtained). In this they proved less than successful. With regard to Anatolia and eastern Thrace, following the creation of a strong and determined Turkish National Movement, and the defeat of Allied (mainly Greek) forces despatched to secure control, the powers were obliged to conclude the Treaty of Lausanne of 24 July 1923, recognising the existence of an independent Turkish state. But they were successful in securing the neutralisation, demilitarisation and internationalisation of the Straits – a principal objective. Similarly with regard to the Arab provinces, where Britain and France, the powers principally concerned, met stiff resistance, they were obliged to modify their plans substantially; though there, in the end, they did succeed in setting up states and governments subject to their own direct or indirect influence or control. Only in the Balkans did they succeed in imposing a settlement without too much difficulty; and even there a number of disputes, in particular that between Italy and Serbia over the future of Fiume and a part of the Adriatic coast, caused considerable delay.

In their efforts to draft a treaty of peace with the Ottoman Empire the Allies proved dilatory in the extreme. Not until February 1920 did they succeed in drafting terms. It was then agreed that, with regard to Anatolia and eastern Thrace, they would seek to impose a settlement that would provide for French and Italian spheres of influence in Cilicia and Lycia; the demilitarisation, neutralisation and internationalisation of the Straits; the creation of an Armenian state, the frontiers of which would be determined by President Wilson, who at one stage had considered accepting an American mandate for Constantinople, the Straits and the Armenian provinces; Greek possession of eastern Thrace, up to the Chataija lines, together with Imbros, Tenedos and, provisionally, after five years, Smyrna; and close allied supervision of whatever Ottoman state would be permitted to survive [3].

During the discussion which preceded the drafting of the peace terms, the British and French considered on a number of occasions the possible expulsion of the Ottomans from Constantinople [*Doc. 31*]. As Lord Curzon, the British Foreign Secretary and principal exponent of a policy of expulsion, pointed out, were they to be left in possession of their capital, then they would quickly embroil the international commission, which it was intended to set up to administer the Straits, in an atmosphere of 'incessant conspiracy and cabal'. In such a situation the 'wily Turk', who for centuries had been a source of 'distraction, intrigue and corruption' in European politics, would find renewed scope for his hereditary talents, whilst 'round the pivots of his own plots would revolve a whirlwind of international intrigue, in which the representatives of all the nations, who still aspired to his inheritance, would eagerly mix' [71, *p. 392*]. In particular Germany and Russia might once again be tempted to intervene, while the Sultan, exploiting the prestige which accompanied the possession of Constantinople, might promote the forces of pan-Islamism and pan-Turanism throughout the east. In the end, however, it was decided that the Ottomans should be permitted to remain. As Edwin Montagu, the Secretary of State for India and a principal opponent of a policy of expulsion, pointed out, the expulsion of the Sultan would be considered a 'grave outrage to Mohammedan sentiment throughout the world, particularly in India' and as others pointed out, it might merely promote 'new and unforeseen complications', including disturbances in Egypt and India and the creation of a Turkey *irredenta* [71, *pp. 392-4*]. Nor would expulsion prevent further German and Russian intervention. On the contrary, by removing the Sultan and his government from the influence and control of the Allies, it might merely promote it. Finally, as the Naval and General Staff advised:

If ... the Sultan and the Turkish Government were removed into Asia Minor, the whole military position would be altered to our disadvantage, for in peace we should lose both knowledge of his plans and power to check his preparations, and the powerful deterrent from evil doing of our having the Sultan and the whole of his Government under our guns would have disappeared. If, therefore, the Sultan and his Government are removed from Constantinople, a much larger garrison would be required, and a more elaborate system of defence, especially on the Asia Minor side, where a veritable frontier, with all its disadvantages and bickering and constant aggravation, would have to be set up [71, *p. 399*].

Curzon was not in any way convinced by these arguments. On 7 January 1920, following the Cabinet meeting at which the decision to maintain the Ottomans in their possession of Constantinople was taken, he wrote:

I ask to place on record my earnest and emphatic dissent from the decision arrived at by the majority of the Cabinet yesterday – in opposition to the advice of the Prime Minister and two successive Foreign Secretaries – to retain the Turk in Constantinople. I believe this to be a short-sighted, and in the long run, a most unfortunate decision.

In order to avoid trouble in India, – largely manufactured and in any case ephemeral, – and to render our task in Egypt less difficult – its difficulty being in reality almost entirely independent of what we may do or not do at Constantinople – we are losing an opportunity for which Europe has waited nearly five centuries, and which may not recur. The idea of a respectable and docile Turkish Government at Constantinople preserved from its hereditary vices by a military cordon of the Powers – including, be it remembered, a permanent British garrison of 10,000 to 15,000 men – is in my judgement a chimera. Nor will it be found that the decision, if carried into effect in Paris, will either solve the Turkish problem or calm the Eastern world.

The Turk at Constantinople must have very different measure meted out to him from the Turk in Konya. He will retain a sovereignty which will have to be a mere simulacrum, and those who have saved him will, unless I am mistaken, presently discover, that his rescue has neither satisfied him nor pacified Islam. But beyond all I regret that the main object for which the war in the East was fought and the sacrifice of Gallipoli endured – namely the liberation of Europe from the Ottoman Turk – has after an almost incredible expenditure of life and treasure been thrown away in the very hour when it has been obtained, and that we shall have left to our descendants – who knows after how much further sacrifice and suffering – a task from which we have flinched [71, *p. 399*].

In the early stages of their discussions the Allies expected that they would be able to impose the terms they had agreed on the Turks without much difficulty. Indeed, a peace treaty incorporating them was signed by representatives of the Allies and the Ottomans at Sèvres on 10 August 1920. By then, however, the situation in Anatolia had changed radically. Not only had the Italians and the Greeks landed forces in southern and western Anatolia in April-May 1919 – the Greek expeditionary force, which the British and French authorised in order to preempt an Italian occupation of the area, landed at Smyrna on 15 May – but also Mustafa Kemal, a high-ranking Ottoman army officer, had succeeded in founding a Turkish National Movement in the interior, capable of imposing its authority throughout the greater part of the subcontinent [62].

That the Turkish Nationalists intended to challenge the power and authority of both the Ottoman Government in Constantinople and the Allies was not long left in doubt. In proclamations published after conferences held in Erzerum and Sivas in July–September 1919, they made it clear that they would accept no peace settlement which did not provide for the complete freedom and independence of those parts of the Ottoman Empire – in effect Anatolia and eastern Thrace, including Constantinople and the Straits – which had re-mained unconquered at the end of the war, and in which Ottoman Muslims formed a majority of the population. They repeated these claims in the National Pact, approved by a newly-elected Ottoman parliament on 28 January 1920, though on this occasion they did admit the need for an international agreement regarding the Straits [*Doc. 32*]. Moreover, in February 1920 Nationalist and irregular forces attacked a French garrison at Marash in Cilicia; and in April-May others, driving elements loyal to the Sultan before them, occupied Balikessir and Adabazar, and advanced menacingly in the direction of Constantinople and the Straits [49].

Faced with this unexpected challenge to their authority, the Allies responded forcefully. On 16 March they occupied Constantinople, which they declared they would hold as a pledge of Turkish good behaviour. A day or so later the Supreme Council agreed to seek the advice of an Allied commission of military and naval experts on the possibility of enforcing the treaty in full. Thereafter, however, Allied determination quickly waned, though in April the Allied leaders did authorise a Greek advance on the Straits in order to clear the Turkish Nationalist forces from the area. In April the Allied commission of experts advised that twenty-seven divisions would be required to execute the treaty in full, and that only nineteen were available, so it was agreed that the Allies should seek merely what Curzon referred to as the 'progressive realisation' of the treaty, in so far as it could be carried out with the forces available. In December, following the return of Constantine, an enemy of the Entente, to the throne of Greece, it was agreed that some modification of the Sèvres treaty might be considered. In February–March 1921, therefore, a conference of the Allied powers was convened in London, to which representatives of the Greek, Ottoman and Turkish Nationalist Governments were invited, to consider possible changes in the treaty, including a favourable revision of the eastern frontier of the proposed Turkish state; a relaxation of the control which it was intended to impose on that state; and a recognition of Turkish sovereignty in Smyrna. The Greeks, however, rejected these proposals out of hand. Moreover, on 23 March, despite the disapproval of the Allies, who declared that henceforth they would remain neutral in the struggle – an area roughly the same size as that occupied by the Allied forces on the Straits was, somewhat optimistically, designated as a 'neutral' zone, which the belligerents were advised to avoid – the Greeks launched an attack on the Turkish Nationalist forces in western Anatolia, capturing Afyonkarahissar, but failing to take Eskishehir. And when, following a Turkish withdrawal to the River Sakarya, they resumed their advance in July–August, they still did not succeed in breaking through. Indeed, after twenty-two days of continuous fighting, they were obliged to abandon the attack and withdraw to defensive positions well to the west. Following the battle, both sides claimed victory, but as Winston Churchill later remarked, the Greeks had involved themselves in a situation where 'anything short of decisive victory was defeat', whilst the Turks were in a position where 'anything short of overwhelming defeat was victory' [12, *pp. 400–2*].

The Greek attempt to resolve the question by force did nothing to strengthen Allied unity. Throughout the struggle the Italians remained bitterly hostile to the Greeks, aiding Turkish irregulars fighting in the Greek zone, while the French suspected that the Greeks were acting merely as surrogates of the British in the area. Nor did the alliance survive unscathed in other respects. In June the Italians concluded an agreement with the Turkish Nationalists, providing for the evacuation of the Italian forces in southern Anatolia. And in October the French, preoccupied with the problem of securing control in Syria, concluded the Franklin-Bouillon Agreement (named after the French diplomat, Henri Franklin-Bouillon, who negotiated it), which provided for the complete evacuation of all French forces in Cilicia [49].

For a time it appeared likely that these agreements, which as Curzon pointed out were in breach of the Treaty of Sèvres, would break the alliance, but in the end, despite heated charges of disloyalty and betrayal, it survived intact. During the following months the Allies continued their search for a negotiated settlement. At a conference held in Paris in March 1922, further substantial modifications of the Sèvres treaty were proposed, including the return of Smyrna to Turkey; the creation of a neutral zone along the Greco-Turkish border in Europe; an adjustment of that border in a sense favourable to the Turks; and a readmission of Turkish sovereignty on the Asiatic shores of the Dardanelles. However, the Turkish Nationalists refused to consider these proposals, except on conditions unacceptable to the Allies, including the immediate evacuation of Smyrna. Moreover, on 26 August 1922, strengthened by their agreements with the French and the Italians, and by substantial Russian support – on 16 March 1921 the Turkish Nationalists and the Bolsheviks, who wished to see the western imperial powers expelled from Turkey, signed a treaty delineating Turkey's frontier in the east and providing for aid on a substantial scale – the Turkish Nationalists launched an attack on the Greek forces in the Afyonkarahissar region, which in a matter of days led to a breakthrough, and in a matter of weeks to the complete expulsion of the Greek expeditionary forces from Anatolia [62].

Following the victory of the Turkish Nationalist forces in Anatolia, the Allied high commissioners in Constantinople at once announced that they would oppose any attempt on the part of the Turkish Nationalists to recover Constantinople, eastern Thrace or the Straits zone by force. During the following weeks, however, as Nationalist forces advanced threateningly on the Allied positions in the area of the Straits, both the French and the Italian governments decided that on no account would they be prepared to risk war merely to secure the temporary preservation of Greek sovereignty in eastern Thrace; and on 18 September, following a series of heated and bitter disputes between the British and the French, in the course of which accusations of betrayal were once again freely exchanged, they withdrew their forces from the Asiatic shores of the Straits. The

British were now isolated, as Commonwealth and Balkan states approached at the time appeared generally unwilling to become involved, and so altered course. At a conference of Allied powers held in Paris on 23 September, it was agreed that Mustafa Kemal should be invited to attend a peace conference, at which a final treaty of peace, providing for a speedy Turkish repossession of eastern Thrace up to the Maritza river, would be concluded. On 11 October, following a further period of acute tension – in the course of which Sir Charles Harington, the commander of the British contingent, tactfully refrained from delivering an ultimatum despatched by the Cabinet, which demanded the instant withdrawal of all Turkish forces in the vicinity of the British lines – an armistice was concluded at Mudania [49].

With the contentious question of eastern Thrace thus satisfactorily resolved, the Allies and the Turkish Nationalists were able, not without difficulty, to reach agreement when they assembled in Lausanne in November to draw up the terms of a final treaty of peace. By the terms of this treaty, which was eventually signed in Lausanne on 24 July 1923, it was agreed that Turkey would concede the loss of Egypt, Cyprus, the Arab provinces and the Dodecanese islands, but would retain possession of Anatolia, including the Armenian provinces, eastern Thrace, Imbros, Tenedos and other islands in the vicinity of the Dardanelles. Only with regard to eastern Thrace and the Straits was there to be any substantial diminution of Turkish sovereignty. In eastern Thrace, a demilitarised zone was to be created, running the length of the Turkish frontier; and in the area of the Straits, a second demilitarised zone would be set up, including the shores of both the Bosphorus and the Dardanelles. The passage of the Straits was henceforth to be administered by an international commission based in Constantinople, and this would provide for the complete freedom of passage of warships and merchant ships in time of peace and in time of war if Turkey remained neutral. If, on the other hand, Turkey were a belligerent in time of war, only the warships and merchant ships of neutrals would enjoy freedom of passage. In order to placate the Russians, however, it was agreed that in time of peace and in time of war, Turkey remaining neutral, the maximum force which any one power might send into the Black Sea should not exceed that of the most powerful fleet in the Black Sea at the time, subject to the proviso that the non-riverain powers might at any time send in a force of not more than three ships, of which no individual ship should exceed 10,000 tonnes [3].

Meanwhile in the Arab provinces Britain and France, the powers principally concerned, proved rather more successful in securing a settlement along the lines envisaged in the Sykes-Picot Agreement. In Syria and Palestine, following the victories of the predominantly British forces, the British commander General Allenby at once established an Occupied Enemy Territory Administration, divided into three zones – a western zone (OETW; originally OET North), consisting of the Syrian littoral, north of Palestine, where it was intended that France would undertake the administration; an eastern zone (OETE), consisting of the interior of Syria and Transjordan, where Faisal would undertake the administration; and a southern zone (OETS), consisting of Palestine west of the Jordan, where, following an agreement concluded by Lloyd George, the British Prime Minister, and Georges Clemenceau, the French Prime Minister, in December 1918, it was agreed that Britain would not only undertake the administration, but also acquire ultimate control. Then in September 1919, following a prolonged period of uncertainty, inspired in part by what the French saw as British prevarication, and in part by the resolution of the Americans to implement the principle of self-determination – in June–July 1919 Woodrow Wilson despatched a commission of enquiry to Syria, to investigate the hopes and expectations of the local populations – the British and French concluded an agreement providing for the evacuation of the British garrisons of OETW and their replacement by French garrisons. At the Conference of San Remo (19–24 April 1920) they agreed that, in accordance with the provisions of the Covenant of the League of Nations, which provided for recognition of the existence of independent nations 'subject to the rendering of administrative advice and assistance by a Mandatory', France should be awarded a mandate for Syria, and Britain mandates for Palestine and Mesopotamia [44].

In the end the French did not remain content merely with direct control of OETW and indirect control of OETE. In July 1920, as Arab national resistance mounted both in OETW and OETE – on 7 March 1920 a Syrian National Congress had claimed independence for the whole of Syria, including Palestine and the Lebanon and elected Faisal king – they despatched a substantial force under the command of General Gouraud into the interior. which, after a battle (little more than a skirmish) at Khan Maysalun, quickly occupied Damascus and placed the whole area under a common administration [123].

In Mesopotamia the government of India had established in the closing stages of the war a quasi-colonial administration, staffed for the most part by British and Indian officials. Shortly after the allocation of the British mandate, the British decided – against the advice, it must be said, of Arnold Wilson, the Acting Civil Commissioner – to seek the creation of a unitary Arab state, ruled over by an Arab head under British tutelage. The frontiers of this state would stretch from the northern boundary of the Mosul vilayet, acquired by Britain in the agreement of December 1918, to the Persian Gulf.

In the event, as Arnold Wilson had predicted, Britain's willingness to placate Arab national sentiment in Mesopotamia proved largely ineffective. Throughout the summer of 1920 Arab unrest mounted, inspired in part by supporters of the Syrian national movement in Damascus – on 8 March Iraqi nationalists in Damascus had had Abdullah, Husain's eldest son, proclaimed King of Iraq. In August insurrection broke out on a considerable scale. As a result, implementation of British policy was for a time delayed. But in November 1920, following the suppression of the insurrection, Sir Percy Cox, who in October had replaced Wilson as Acting Civil Commissioner, succeeded in persuading a number of Iraqi notables – including Sayyid Talib of Basra and Jafar Pasha al-Askari – to form a government, which was led by Said Abd al Rahman al Gaylani, Naqib of Baghdad; and on 11 July 1921 the Council of State was persuaded to pass an unanimous resolution declaring Faisal, recently expelled from Damascus, king [44].

Arab discontent also found expression in Palestine. Provoked by the unwillingness of the Allies to admit the claims of the Syrian nationalists to complete independence, and by Jewish demands for unrestricted immigration, militant Arabs formed liberation societies and attacked Jewish settlements and communities. Following the Supreme Council decision to grant Britain a mandate for Palestine, these attacks increased both in frequency and intensity, as they did again when on 1 July 1920 the British established a civil administration, headed by a high commissioner, Sir Herbert Samuel [*Doc. 33*]. However, the fact that in January 1919 Faisal felt able to conclude an agreement with Dr Chaim Weizmann, the Zionist leader, would suggest that in the period immediately following the First World War at least, Arab – though not necessarily Palestinian Arab – resentment was by no means as intense as it was later to become [83].

The installation of a British administration in Palestine did not conclude the Allied task of creating a new order in the Middle East.

In February 1921 Abdullah, intent on raising a rebellion against the French in Syria, entered Transjordan and assumed control of the administration there. The British, who continued to feel a debt of gratitude to the Hashemites for their support in the war, recognised him as ruler, on condition merely that he should abandon his intention of attacking the French. In this inconsequential way was the Emirate of Transjordan, later Jordan, created.

Meanwhile in the Balkans, where the western Entente powers endeavoured for the most part to reward friends and punish enemies, significant changes were enacted. By the Treaty of Saint Germain (10 September 1919), Austria was made to cede substantial territories, including Bosnia, Herzegovina and Dalmatia, to Serbia, now transformed into the South Slav Kingdom of Yugoslavia. By the Treaty of Trianon (4 June 1920), Hungary was made to cede Transylvania and the Bukovina to Romania, which in the closing months of the war also recovered Bessarabia; and by the Treaty of Neuilly (27 November 1919), Bulgaria was made to cede the Dobrudja to Romania, and western Thrace to Greece. As for the port of Fiume, following a prolonged dispute between Italy and Yugoslavia, it fell eventually to Italy.

PART THREE: ASSESSMENT

11 THE GREAT POWERS AND THE OTTOMAN EMPIRE

It is evident that many particular questions fell under the general heading of the Eastern Question. These included the great strategic questions of the control of the Balkans, the Turkish Straits and the Near and Middle Eastern routes to India and the east; the rise of nationalism, first in the Balkans and then in Anatolia and the Arab provinces; the economic interests of the powers in the Ottoman Empire, in particular those of Britain, France, Italy, and, towards the end of the nineteenth century, Germany; the protection of the Sultan's Greek Orthodox and Catholic subjects, and the related question of the administration of the Holy Places; and, finally, the territorial ambitions of the powers, in particular those of Russia and Austria in the Balkans and those of France and Italy in the Levant and North Africa.

Throughout the late eighteenth, nineteenth and early twentieth centuries, these questions provoked a series of crises, caused for the most part by either the decline of Ottoman power or the advance of one or other of the Great Powers in the area. Thus in the second half of the eighteenth century Russia and the Ottoman Empire fought a series of wars for the control of the northern shores of the Black Sea. In the nineteenth century the subject peoples of the Balkans, led by the Serbs and Greeks, rose in revolt against the Ottomans, while in the Arab provinces the expansionary policies adopted by Mehmet Ali, the ruler of Egypt, led twice to war. In the 1850s a dispute regarding the protection of Greek Orthodox and Latin Christians and the administration of the Holy Places led rapidly to war between Russia and the Ottoman Empire, and in the 1870s Ottoman maladministration in the Balkans helped to provoke yet another Russo–Turkish war. Again in the 1870s the bankruptcy of both the Ottoman Empire and Egypt provoked major financial crises, whilst in the opening years of the twentieth century ambitious schemes of railway construction, undertaken by the Germans in the Ottoman Empire, led to a series of disputes regarding the economic interests of the powers. Finally, frontier disputes between Russia and the Ottoman Empire regarding the possession of territory in eastern Anatolia and the Caucasus played a part in provoking war on a number of occasions, while Italy's seizure of Tripolitania in 1911 led to an immediate outbreak of hostilities.

Such questions alone, however, and the disputes to which they gave rise, did not constitute the Eastern Question. What united them into a single composite whole was the fact that each was seen by one or other of the powers, and occasionally by all, as involving, or at least threatening, a change in the balance of power, both in Europe, and – a matter of major significance for Britain, in particular – in Asia, and even in the world. Thus when France in the French Revolutionary and Napoleonic Wars endeavoured to overturn the balance of power both in Europe and in Asia, the other Great Powers joined in a series of coalitions aimed at her containment. When Russia, in the first Mehmet Ali crisis, threatened to establish a predominant position at Constantinople and secure control of the Turkish Straits, Britain and France took steps to oppose her. They did so more forcefully during the Crimean War, when Russia once again sought to extend her influence in the Ottoman Empire. Again, in the Eastern Crisis of 1875–78, the western powers, with the possible exception of Germany, were united in their determination to prevent a further extension of Russian power in the Balkans; and in the First World War, when the Central Powers in conjunction with the Ottoman Empire attempted to bring about a fundamental change in the balance of power both in Europe and the world, the powers of the Triple Entente, later joined by Italy, united against them.

The response of the Great Powers to the conflicts generated by the Eastern Question and the threat to the balance of power which they entailed, was, despite frequent talk of partition, generally conservative. Throughout the greater part of the nineteenth century they were motivated primarily by considerations of defence – for Austria the need to preserve the *status quo* in the Balkans; for Russia the need to secure the closure of the Straits; and for Britain and France the need to protect the Near and Middle Eastern routes to India and the east against the threat posed by the advance of Russia – and they sought to maintain the independence and integrity of the Ottoman Empire. When a dispute arose which threatened that independence, they usually sought to resolve it by negotiation rather than by war. Thus at the Congress of Vienna (1815), when the representatives of the powers assembled to make peace with France, it was agreed that they would seek to preserve the independence and integrity of the Ottoman Empire (though they failed to incorporate a clause to this effect in the treaty); and in the 1820s when the Greeks rose in revolt, the powers endeavoured, in the early stages of the dispute at least, to secure a settlement which would as far as possible underpin the *status quo*. Again, in the second Mehmet Ali Crisis of 1839–41, when the representatives of Britain, Austria and Russia assembled in London to decide on a policy, it was agreed that any action they might take should be animated by the desire to 'maintain the integrity and independence of the Ottoman Empire as a security for the peace of Europe' [1]. After the Crimean War – the only occasion on which a dispute between the Great Powers regarding the Eastern Question led to a major European conflict – when the representatives of the powers assembled in Paris to draft a peace treaty, they agreed not only to secure the independence and integrity of the Ottoman Empire through effectual and reciprocal guarantes, but also to allow the Ottoman Empire to 'participate in the advantages of the public law and system (*concert*) of Europe' [*Doc. 18*]. Finally, at the Congress of Berlin, the last of the great conferences convened to settle the affairs of Europe, the powers, in particular Britain and France, were at pains to preserve the integrity of what remained of the Ottoman Empire. Only in the First World War, when the Ottoman Empire joined with the Central Powers in an attempt to achieve a fundamental change in the balance of power both in Europe and in the world, were Britain, France and Russia obliged to abandon this policy. Even then many people, in Britain at least, would have preferred to preserve the Ottoman Empire as a barrier against future Russian, French or German expansion in the area.

It should not be assumed, however, that the powers remained invariably committed to the preservation of the *status quo*. In the Greek War of Independence their collective action at Navarino effectively undermined the capacity of the Sultan to re-establish his authority in the Morea. In the later 1830s the Russians seriously considered a seizure of Constantinople and the Straits; and in the 1850s and 1870s they actually instituted forward policies seriously threatening the independence and integrity of the Ottoman Empire. The Austrians likewise considered on several occasions instituting a forward policy in the western Balkans; and in 1908 they annexed Bosnia and Herzegovina, thereby sparking off a diplomatic crisis that played a significant part in the causation of the First World War. As for the British, despite their commitment to the pre-servation of the *status quo*, they permitted themselves to be provoked, willy-nilly, into undertaking an occupation of Egypt, which further undermined confidence in the future survival of the Ottoman Empire. And the Italians, who remained perhaps the least committed of all the Great Powers to the preservation of the Ottoman Empire, simply seized Tripolitania in 1911. Thus individually and even at times collectively, the powers undermined the policy to which to a greater or lesser extent they were committed, and further hastened the demise of the Ottoman Empire, whose stamina, despite all prognostications to the contrary, remained remarkable to the end.

It would be a mistake to conclude, as a number of historians have done, that contemporary statesmen exaggerated the significance of the Eastern Question and the international rivalries that it provoked. Throughout the nineteenth century, particularly in the later years, the interest of Russia and Austria in the fate of the Balkans, of Britain, France and Russia in the regime governing the Straits, and of Britain and France in the Near and Middle Eastern routes to India and the east, remained of overriding importance, capable at any moment of provoking a European war. It is however true that, as long as the policies adopted by the powers were motivated primarily by considerations of defence – as long, in other words, as no power adopted a forward policy, seeking a radical change in the balance of power: a situation which prevailed throughout the greater part of the nineteenth century – the threat posed by the Eastern Question to the peace of Europe was less significant than it might otherwise have been.

12 THE AFTERMATH

Following the final collapse and partition of the Ottoman Empire, Great-Power conflict in the Near and Middle East continued unabated. With regard to the Balkans, Soviet demands, presented in November 1940, that the USSR should acquire an exclusive sphere of influence in Bulgaria and the area of the Straits, in return for Russia's adhesion to the Three-Power Pact (Germany, Italy and Japan), played a significant, perhaps even a decisive, part in persuading Hitler to opt for war with the Soviet Union, thereby securing not only his own defeat and the partition of Germany, but also Russian control of the greater part of eastern Europe and the Balkans, including Hungary, Romania and Bulgaria. In the period immediately following the war the Russians did not abandon their demands for bases on the Straits, the granting of which, as a number of commentators noted at the time, would have placed Turkey, and possibly Greece, in the Russian sphere of influence. Only British opposition, and the unexpected intervention of the United States in the dispute, which later gave rise to American guarantees regarding the defence of Turkey and Greece, persuaded the Russians to desist.

For Britain, which in the 1930s had re-established good relations with Turkey, Turkish neutrality in the Second World War brought advantages of incalculable value, including the protection of British interests (now including oil) in the Middle East against an attack mounted from the Balkans. At the same time the strong position established by Britain in the Arab world enabled the British to repel attacks mounted by German and Italian forces in North Africa; though in the early, critical stages of the war, Arab dissension, particularly in Egypt, Iraq and Palestine, caused considerable difficulty. In Egypt – where in 1922, following nationalist riots, the British had unilaterally revoked the protectorate and proclaimed independence, subject to reservations regarding the security of imperial communications and defence; and where in 1936 they had concluded a treaty providing for a withdrawal of British forces to the Canal zone – the Egyptian people and their rulers remained generally hostile; though fears that following an Axis victory Italy or Germany might take over caused considerable concern. In Iraq – where in 1930 Britain had concluded a treaty of alliance, providing for the independence of Iraq and its admission to the League of Nations, subject again to reservations regarding foreign policy and defence – Allied defeats in the Balkans and North Africa were followed almost at once by the overthrow of the pro-British government, approaches to the Axis powers for military assistance, and acts of resistance against the British garrison. Following the arrival of reinforcements from India, Palestine and Transjordan, this resistance was quickly suppressed; but it nonetheless posed for a time a serious threat to British interests in the area. Finally, in Palestine, where Britain's responsibility for the implementation of the Balfour Declaration caused considerable resentment, Arab opinion remained generally hostile; though British appeasement, in the form of tighter immigration controls introduced in 1939, did succeed for a time in reducing tension.

For the French and Italians, on the other hand, the Second World War spelt disaster. In Syria and Lebanon – Lebanon, one of four divisions of the mandated territory, rapidly acquired an autonomous status – where in the inter-war years nationalist resistance, including at times open rebellion, had continued, the defeat of France led first to a British occupation, and then, following Free French proclamations of independence and a prolonged nationalist struggle, to complete independence, which was recognised in 1945 by the international community, including France. In Libya, a British military administration was established following the defeat of the Axis forces; and in 1951, following a prolonged Great-Power struggle regarding the future of the country, an independent kingdom was created, ruled over by King Idris, a leader of the resistance.

In the period following the Second World War, the British did not long retain the predominant position they had established in the Arab world. In 1948, following a renewal of the inter-communal strife which had characterised the inter-war years, and a campaign of terror mounted by Zionist groups, they officially terminated their mandate for Palestine, and evacuated their forces, leaving the Jews to defend the state of Israel, proclaimed on 14 May. Likewise in 1954, since Britain's evacuation of India had considerably reduced the importance of the Suez Canal to the British Empire – though the increasing quantities of oil passing through the Canal in the post-war period counterbalanced this decline to some extent – the British concluded an agreement with the revolutionary regime recently established in Egypt by a group of Arab army officers, led by Gamal Abdul Nasser, providing for a withdrawal of British forces from the Canal zone, subject to a provision that they might return in the event of an attack on Egypt or on a member of the Arab League by an outside power. Nor, following Nasser's nationalisation of the Canal, did an attempt made in conjunction with the French in 1956 to reoccupy the Canal zone succeed. On the contrary, it served merely to undermine further Britain's declining prestige in the Arab world, and to enhance Nasser's. During the following years, therefore, Nasser was enabled to mount a successful pan-Arab offensive, which in 1958 led to a union of Egypt and Syria, later aborted, and to the collapse of the Hashemite regime in Iraq. Finally, in 1971, the British withdrew their remaining forces from the Persian Gulf, thereby ending a century and more of direct political and military involvement in the area.

PART FOUR: DOCUMENTS

DOCUMENT 1   THE TREATY OF KUTCHUK KAINARDJI,
             21 JULY 1774

Article 111, which was bitterly resented by the Turks, laid the foundation for Russian annexation of the Crimea. Article VII was frequently referred to by the Russians in their dispute with the Ottomans in the period preceding the Crimean War.

Article III. All the Tartar peoples – those of the Crimea, of the Budjiac, of the Kuban, the Edissans, the Geambouiluks and Editschkuls – shall, without any exception, be acknowledged by the two Empires as free nations, and entirely independent of every foreign Power, governed by their own Sovereign, of the race of Genghis Khan, elected and raised to the throne by all the Tartar peoples; which Sovereign shall govern them according to their ancient laws and usages, being responsible to no foreign Power whatsoever; for which reason, neither the Court of Russia nor the Ottoman Porte shall interfere, under any pretext whatever, with the election of the said Khan, or in the domestic, political, civil and internal affairs of the same; but, on the contrary, they shall acknowledge and consider the said Tartar nation, in its political and civil state, upon the same footing as the other Powers who are governed by themselves, and are dependent upon God alone. As to the ceremonies of religion, as the Tartars profess the same faith as the Mahometans, they shall regulate themselves, with respect to His Highness, in his capacity of Grand Caliph of Mahometanism, according to the precepts prescribed to them by their law, without compromising, nevertheless, the stability of their political and civil liberty ...

Article VII. The Sublime Porte promises to protect constantly the Christian religion and its churches, and it also allows the Minister of the Imperial Court of Russia to make, upon all occasions, representations, as well in favour of the new church at Constantinople, of which mention will be made in Article XIV, as on behalf of its officiating ministers, promising to take such representations into consideration, as being made by a confidential functionary of a neighbouring and sincerely friendly Power ...

Article XI. For the convenience and advantage of the two Empires, there shall be a free and unimpeded navigation for the merchant-ships belonging to the two Contracting Powers, in all the seas which wash their shores; the Sublime Porte grants to Russian merchant-vessels, namely, such as are universally employed by the other Powers for commerce and in the ports, a free passage from the Black Sea into the White Sea; and reciprocally from the White Sea into the Black Sea, as also the power of entering all the ports and harbours situated either on the sea-coasts, or in the passages and channels which join those seas.

Anderson, [4], pp. 9–11.

DOCUMENT 2   **DECREE OF THE DIRECTORY ORDERING GENERAL BONAPARTE TO LAUNCH THE EGYPTIAN CAMPAIGN, 12 APRIL 1798**

The British occupation of the Cape of Good Hope, referred to by the Directory, took place in 1795.

The Executive Directory
Considering that the Beys who have seized the government of Egypt have established the most intimate ties with the English and have placed themselves under their absolute dependence; that in consequence they have engaged in the most open hostilities and most horrible cruelties against the French whom they vex, pillage and murder daily;

Considering that it is its duty to pursue the enemies of the Republic wherever they may be and in any place where they engage in hostile activities;

Considering, in addition, that the infamous treason with the help of which Britain became mistress of the Cape of Good Hope has rendered access to India by the customary route very difficult to the vessels of the Republic, it is important to open to the Republican forces another route thither, to combat the satellites of the English Government and dry up the source of its corrupting riches;

Decrees as follows:

Article 1. The General-in-chief of the army of the East shall direct the land and sea forces whose command is entrusted to him to Egypt and shall take possession of that country.

Article 2. He shall drive the English from all their possessions in the Orient which he can reach and shall in particular destroy all their factories on the Red Sea.

Article 3. He shall have the Isthmus of Suez cut and shall take all necessary measures to ensure to the French Republic the free and exclusive possession of the Red Sea.

Article 4. He shall improve by all the means at his disposal the position of the natives of Egypt.

Article 5. He shall maintain, in so far as this depends on him, a good understanding with the Grand Seigneur and his immediate subjects.

Article 6. The present decree shall not be printed.

Correspondance de Napoleon Ier, iv, Paris, 1860, pp. 69–71.

DOCUMENT 3   A BRITISH VIEW OF THE OTTOMAN EMPIRE IN 1802

In a letter written on 29 November 1802, in response to an enquiry from Sir Hugh Inglis, a director of the East India Company, Harford Jones, the British consul in Baghdad, considered the probable consequences of a dissolution of the Ottoman Empire.

My situation and the duties of my office have caused me to reflect on the probable consequences of the dissolution of the Turkish Empire; and the information I have obtained from channels not accessible to many makes me think a great revolution in the Turkish Empire is near at hand, unless, as you observe, the period of it shall be protracted by some fortunate and unforeseen event. In order to make myself more clearly understood, I shall class the accidents which to me seem probable soon to arrive to the Turkish Empire under separate heads.

Radical dissolution of the Empire, by the Turks being driven out of Europe by force – I am very far from considering that the latter case necessarily comprises the former. The manner in which the spiritual and temporal powers are blended in the person of the Ottoman Emperor has not been considered with proper attention; for it is by the intimate connexion of these powers that the Turkish Empire has been kept so long from falling; since every Sunny who rebels against the Imam (the Grand Signor) renders his marriage null. A Pacha, therefore, always affects to relieve the Imam from evil ministers, but never professes to take up arms against his person. The House of Othman can never lose the Imamet but by a renunciation forced or upheld in favour of some powerful Mussulman family. As long as the House of Othman possesses this office, the allegiance of every Sunny being due to it, though the Prince may be changed, in consequence of certain canonical disqualifications, real or pretended, there cannot be a radical dissolution of the Turkish Empire by any European power.

The Ottoman Emperor takes the title of Guardian of the Holy Cities (Mecca and Medina); and, as it was obtained by Selim at the same time with the Imamet, there are some doubts whether the loss of the former does not imply that of the latter. However, I consider it as most probable that, the guardianship of these cities being by force transferred to any other Mahomedan prince, would deprive the Ottoman Prince of so great a part of his sanctity, that he would soon be obliged to make a renunciation of the Imamet in favour of the victor. Here, then, would certainly be what I should call a radical dissolution of the Turkish Empire: but what bound the old Turkish Empire together would cement the new Tartar or probably Arabian Empire, which would start up in its place.

But, as the powers forming such a league will probably include in their designs a part of Asiatic Turkey, the change of manners and sentiments in those quarters may render the great Pachas negligent both of their spiritual and temporal obedience, when they find the Caliph Sultan too weak to save the Empire. In this case the head of the Ottoman House may become a mere pageant, and that part of the Turkish Empire unpossessed by the European powers may split into independent principalities.

It is to this situation of things my opinion inclines, because, in looking through Asia, I see no Mahomedan power or family to take the place of the Ottoman Emperor. Before, however, I offer my opinion on this subject, I will advert to your question of – What would become of Egypt? If we could not keep it ourselves, I should think it were better that any European power possessed it than the French or the Mamelukes (in the end, another name for a French Government), for, having means of supporting a communication with the Mamelukes greater than those of Great Britain, and near 4,000 having passed into France, who might be sent to their native soil as agents of the French, that influence would necessarily preponderate.

Considering Egypt in our hands as, for many years, a drain of both money and men, if any security could be obtained that it would not become a channel through which India might be attacked, I should think that we had effected all that true policy required; and, at all events, we might insist on retaining Makinga, which to us, as the leading maritime power, may be called the key of Egypt. ...

C. W. Vane (ed.), *Correspondence of Viscount Castlereagh*, second series, v, William Shoberl, 1851, pp. 173–5.

DOCUMENT 4   CZARTORYSKI ON THE FUTURE OF THE
OTTOMAN EMPIRE, 29 FEBRUARY 1804

*Prince Czartoryski, a close associate of Tsar Alexander I, became Deputy
Minister for Foreign Affairs in January 1804.*

There is no doubt that the Ottoman Empire threatens to collapse and that
its future fate touches on the most essential interests of Russia. It is
therefore urgent that our court should draw up a plan on this important
subject in which every possible and probable case is foreseen, so that we can
see clearly where we are going and proceed with assurance towards an
immediate or eventual objective, according to the course taken by events.
Our objective at the moment cannot be other than that of preserving the
Ottoman Empire in its present state and hindering its partition. The
advantage of having a weak and peaceful neighbour, and the facilities which
our trade on the Black Sea has recently obtained, are sufficient reasons for
contenting ourselves with the present state of affairs and preferring it to any
opportunities which the future might offer and of which the consequences
must always be to some extent uncertain. However I must point out that the
facilities which the Black Sea trade has obtained, and which are for the
Russian empire an object of the highest importance, result only from the
extreme weakness of the Turkish government and from the quite unique
circumstances produced by the war of the revolution. As a result, the
facilities and the incalculable advantages in power and prosperity which
may result from them must still be regarded as not entirely assured since we
should lose them as soon as the Porte succeeded in regaining its former
strength or if, intimidated by the threats of the French government, led
astray by its cunning promises, it changed its policy and threw itself into the
arms of France, or if finally any European power succeeded in taking
possession of Greece, of its archipelago and soon afterwards of
Constantinople. It is easy to see that, in this last case above all, the safety of
the Russian Empire would be deeply compromised and one of the most
essential outlets for her trade would find itself at the mercy of another
power. Supposing that the Turkish government, forgetting its deep-rooted
jealousy towards us and convinced of the danger it runs in lending itself to
the projects of the French, should remain faithfully attached to Russia and
unite sincerely with her if Bonaparte carries out his attack upon it, the
safety and the fate of the Ottoman Empire will nevertheless remain very
uncertain. ...

Anderson, [4], pp. 23–5.

DOCUMENT 5   A BRITISH VIEW OF THE AGREEMENT
CONCLUDED AT TILSIT IN 1807

*On 11 October 1808, Sir Robert Adair, a British diplomat, wrote to the
Reis Effendi (the Ottoman Foreign Minister) regarding the agreement
concluded by Napoleon and Tsar Nicholas I at Tilsit.*

The Ottoman Government well knows the nature of the engagements
entered into between France and Russia at the peace of Tillsitt [*sic*]. It
cannot be ignorant that through the prevalence of the influence of France,
an eventual partition of European Turkey was then determined upon. The
double and perfidious part acted by Bonaparte upon that occasion has long
been manifest. An article in the ostensible treaty stipulated for the
evacuation of Moldavia and Wallachia by the Russian troops. This stipulation he boasted to the Sublime Porte that he had dictated to Russia in his
quality of ally and protector of the integrity of the Ottoman empire. But the
truth could not long be disguised. The secret of the engagements made at
Tillsitt was communicated to your Government, and the Sublime Porte was
then enabled to see that this article, which Bonaparte pretended to have
extorted with so much difficulty from Russia, instead of being a stipulation
to prevent the dismemberment of your provinces, was, in fact, an
arrangement to regulate the manner of taking possession of them. So far
from its evincing any regard for the safety of the Ottoman Empire, it was a
proof of nothing more than his distrust of his new confederate Russia,
whom he would not suffer to remain in possession of the provinces allotted
to her in the plan of partition before he should be in a condition to seize
upon those which he had allotted to himself. ...

R. Adair, *The Negotiations for the Peace of the Dardanelles*, Longman,
1845, i, p. 37.

DOCUMENT 6   ALEXANDER YPSILANTIS'S
PROCLAMATION OF REVOLT, 24
FEBRUARY 1821

*The 'Mighty Empire' referred to in the proclamation was undoubtedly
Russia.*

Fight for Faith and Motherland! The time has come, O Hellenes. Long ago
the people of Europe, fighting for their own rights and liberties, invited us
to imitation. These although partially free tried with all their strength to
increase their freedom and through this all their prosperity.

Our brethren and friends are everywhere ready. The Serbs, the Souliots and the whole of Epirus, bearing arms, await us. Let us then unite with enthusiasm. The Motherland is calling us!

Europe, fixing its eyes upon us, wonders at our inertia. Let all the mountains of Greece resound, therefore, with the echo of our battle trumpet, and the valleys with the fearful clash of our arms. Europe will admire our valour. Our tyrants, trembling and pale, will flee before us.

The enlightened peoples of Europe are occupied in restoring the same well-being, and, full of gratitude for the benefactions of our forefathers towards them, desire the liberation of Greece. We, seemingly worthy of ancestral virtue and of the present century, are hopeful that we will achieve their defence and help. Many of these freedom-lovers want to come and fight alongside us. Move, O friends, and you will see a Mighty Empire defend our rights! You will see even many of our enemies, moved by our just cause, turn their backs to the enemy and unite with us. Let them approach with a sincere spirit. The Motherland will embrace them! Who then hinders your manly arms? Our cowardly enemy is sick and weak. Our generals are experienced, and all our fellow countrymen are full of enthusiasm. Unite, then, O brave and magnanimous Greeks! Let national phalanxes be formed, let patriotic legions appear and you will see those old giants of despotism fall by themselves, before our triumphant banners.

R. Clogg, *The Movement for Greek Independence*, Macmillan, 1976, p. 201.

DOCUMENT 7 **REPORT OF A RUSSIAN SPECIAL COMMITTEE ON THE AFFAIRS OF TURKEY, 16 SEPTEMBER 1829**

The committee, chaired by Count Kochubei, was set up by Tsar Nicholas I to consider future Russian policy in the Near East.

After having heard the reading of these various documents the Committee first of all thoroughly examined the situation of Russia in the grave circumstances of the moment and the course which her true interests command her to follow with regard to the Ottoman Empire. Impressed by the force and obviousness of the arguments developed in the documents submitted to the Committee by the Ministry of foreign affairs [*sic*], and struck above all by the justness of the considerations contained in the memorandum of privy [*sic*] Councillor Daschkoff [Dashkov]; in which the advantages and difficulties resulting for Russia from the neighbourhood of a state such as the Ottoman Empire are indicated and weighed against one another, the Committee unanimously recognized:

That the advantages of maintaining the Ottoman Empire in Europe are greater than the difficulties which it presents.

That its fall would henceforth be contrary to the true interests of Russia.

That as a result it would be prudent to seek to prevent it, by taking advantage of all opportunities which may still present themselves to conclude an honourable peace. . .

In case therefore of this catastrophe [i.e., the fall of the Ottoman Empire], which we should be conscious of having sought to prevent by all the means in our power, taking place, as in that in which the Sultan, having taken refuge in Asia, continued to refuse our proposals and thus deprived himself of His States in Europe, it would become urgent to take certain provisional decisions on which the Committee has also been asked to deliberate. After examining those, which have already been prescribed by HIS MAJESTY THE EMPEROR to the Commander in Chief, as well as the measures proposed by the Ministry of foreign affairs, the Committee has agreed:

1. That Turkey in Europe would be occupied militarily by the Russian armies, until the fate of the countries which compose it should be definitively decided.

2. That this occupation should be made as imposing as possible.

3. That to this end Constantinople, the Castles of the Bosphorus and those of the Dardanelles shall have Russian garrisons.

4. That Widdin and some fortified points in Servia should be occupied by our troops.

5. That in no case should Belgrade be occupied by Russian troops, and that if the Turks were driven from it, this frontier fortress should be garrisoned by Servians.

6. That all other measures which the General in Chief may judge necessary to guarantee the safety of the army during the occupation, as well as the maintenance of public order, should be left to his prudence and solicitude. Complete latitude is granted him on this subject.

7. With relation to the diplomatic course to be followed, the Committee recognises:

That it would be contrary to all the rules of a sane policy to decide arbitrarily and without the agreement of the principal Powers the state of affairs which should replace the Ottoman Empire in Europe.

Anderson, [4], pp. 35–9.

DOCUMENT 8   METTERNICH ON THE OTTOMAN EMPIRE AS A NEIGHBOUR

Metternich pointed out the advantages of having the Ottoman Empire as a neighbour in a letter to Prince Paul Esterhazy, the Austrian Ambassador in London, on 2 December 1828.

We look on the Ottoman Empire as the best of our neighbours: since she is scrupulously true to her word, we regard contact with her as equivalent to contact with a natural frontier which never claims our attention or dissipates our energies. We look on Turkey as the last bastion standing in the way of the expansion of another Power ...

G. de Bertier de Sauvigny, *Metternich and His Times*, Darton, Longman and Todd, 1962, p. 247.

DOCUMENT 9   METTERNICH ON THE GREEK QUESTION

Metternich considered the implications of Greek nationalism in a letter to Esterhazy, dated 21 September 1829.

What do we mean by the *Greeks*? Do we mean a people, a country, or a religion? If either of the first two, where are the dynastic and geographical boundaries? If the third, then upwards of fifty million men are Greeks: the Austrian Empire alone embraces five million of them ... the Emperor, our August Master, will never consent that the Greeks, his subjects, should consider themselves at the same time to be citizens of the new Greece. In this respect he can only follow the rules of public justice which prevent him from considering his Milanese and Venetian subjects as members of an Italian body politic, or his Galician subjects as belonging to a kingdom of Poland. Long experience has taught us to realize that in racial denominations there may lie elements of trouble between empires and bones of contention between people and governments. And what a powerful and ever hostile weapon such denominations become in the hands of those who overthrow, or seek to overthrow, the existing order!

G. de Bertier de Sauvigny, *Metternich and His Times*, Darton, Longman and Todd, 1962, p. 35.

DOCUMENT 10   THE TREATY OF HUNKIAR ISKELESI, 8 JULY 1833

The secret and separate article, which caused such concern in Britain and France, did not in fact grant Russia free passage of the Straits.

Article 1. There shall be for ever peace, amity and alliance between His Majesty the Emperor of all the Russias and His Majesty the Emperor of the Ottomans, their empires and their subjects, as well by land as by sea. This alliance having solely for its object the common defence of their dominions against all attack, their Majesties engage to come to an unreserved understanding with each other upon all the matters which concern their respective tranquillity and safety, and to afford to each other mutually for this purpose substantial aid, and the most efficacious assistance.

Article 2. The Treaty of Peace concluded at Adrianople, on the 14th of September 1829, as well as all the other Treaties comprised therein, as also the Convention signed at St Petersburg, on the 14th of April 1830, and the arrangement relating to Greece concluded at Constantinople, on the 9th and 21st July 1832, are fully confirmed by the present Treaty of Defensive Alliance, in the same manner as if the said transactions had been inserted in it word for word.

Article 3. In consequence of the principle of conservation and mutual defence, which is the basis of the present Treaty of Alliance, and by reason of a most sincere desire of securing the permanence, maintenance and entire independence of the Sublime Porte, his Majesty the Emperor of all the Russias, in the event of circumstances occurring which should again determine the Sublime Porte to call for the naval and military assistance of Russia ... engages to furnish, by land and by sea, as many troops and forces as the two high contracting parties may deem necessary. It is accordingly agreed, that in this case the land and sea forces, whose aid the Sublime Porte may call for, shall be held at its disposal ...

Article 5. Although the two high contracting parties sincerely intend to maintain this engagement to the most distant period of time, yet, as it is possible that in process of time circumstances may require that some changes should be made in this Treaty, it has been agreed to fix its duration at eight years from the day of the exchange of the Imperial Ratifications. The two parties, previously to the expiration of that term, will concert together, according to the state of affairs at that time, as to the renewal of the said Treaty ...

SEPARATE ARTICLE

In virtue of one of the clauses of the first Article of the Patent Treaty of Defensive Alliance concluded between the Imperial Court of Russia and the Sublime Porte, the two high contracting parties are bound to afford to each other mutually substantial aid, and the most efficacious assistance for the safety of their respective dominions. Nevertheless, as his Majesty the Emperor of all the Russias, wishing to spare the Sublime Ottoman Porte the expense and inconvenience which might be occasioned to it, by affording substantial aid, will not ask for that aid if circumstances should place the Sublime Porte under the obligation of furnishing it, the Sublime Ottoman Porte, in the place of the aid which it is bound to furnish in case of need, according to the principle of reciprocity of the Patent Treaty, shall confine its action in favour of the Imperial Court of Russia to closing the strait of the Dardanelles, that is to say, to not allowing any foreign vessels of war to enter therein under any pretext whatsoever.

Anderson, [4], pp. 42–3.

DOCUMENT 11   THE RUSSIAN POSITION ON THE SECOND MEHMET ALI CRISIS, 1839

Nesselrode, the Russian Foreign Minister, advised Count Pozzo di Borgo, the Russian Ambassador in Paris, of his thinking regarding the second Mehmet Ali Crisis in a despatch composed on 15 June 1839.

The real danger for Europe at large is not in a combat carried on in Syria between the troops of the Sultan and those of the Pasha of Egypt.

Neither would there be danger to Europe if the Sultan succeeded in reconquering Syria, as he wishes and hopes to do. The danger would not begin to become serious until, in the event of the fate of arms declaring against the Sultan, the Pasha of Egypt should profit by this advantage to place the safety of Constantinople and the existence of the Ottoman Empire in peril ...

To prevent things reaching such a point, it is of consequence to take measures in time to confine the struggle between the Sultan and Mehmet Ali within certain limits, in order that this struggle may in no case extend itself so as to compromise the safety of the capital of the Ottoman Empire.

With this view, it has appeared to us essential to come to an understanding, frankly, with the Great Powers of Europe who, equally with us, have at heart to prevent the danger which we have just pointed out. Among those Powers Great Britain is incontestably the one that can exercise the greatest influence over the fate of this question, and can cooperate in the most decisive manner in realising the pacific intentions of our august Master.

Anderson, [4], pp. 45–6.

DOCUMENT 12   THE BRITISH POSITION ON THE SECOND MEHMET ALI CRISIS, 1839

Palmerston set out the British position in a letter to Viscount Beauvale, the British Ambassador in Vienna, on 28 June 1839.

The general view which Her Majesty's Government, as at present informed, entertain of the affair in question, may be stated as follows:

The Great Powers are justified in interfering in these matters, which are, in fact, a contest between a sovereign and his subject, because this contest threatens to produce great and imminent danger to the deepest interests of other Powers, and to the general peace of Europe. Those interests and that peace require the maintenance of the Turkish Empire; and the maintenance of the Turkish Empire is, therefore, the primary object to be aimed at. This object cannot be secured without putting an end to future chances of collision between the Sultan and Mehemet Ali. But as long as Mehemet Ali continues to occupy Syria, there will be danger of such collision. Mehemet Ali cannot hold Syria without a large military force constantly stationed there. As long as there is an Egyptian force in Syria, there must necessarily be a Turkish army in that part of Asia Minor which borders on Syria. Each party might agree at present to reduce those forces to a given amount, but neither could be sure that the other was not, after a time, secretly increasing his amount of force; and each party would, beyond a doubt, gradually augment his own force; and thus at no distant period, the same state of things which has existed of late, would again recur: for the motives and passions which have led to it would still be in action. Mehemet Ali, or Ibrahim, would still desire to add more territory to their Pashalics; the Sultan would still burn to drive them back into Egypt.

It appears then to Her Majesty's Government, that there can be no end to the danger with which these affairs menace the peace of Europe until Mehemet Ali shall have restored Syria to the direct authority of the Sultan; shall have retired into Egypt; and shall have interposed the Desert between his troops and authorities and the troops and authorities of the Sultan. But Mehemet Ali could not be expected to consent to this, unless some equivalent advantage were granted to him; and this equivalent advantage might be hereditary succession in his family to the Pashalic of Egypt: Mehemet Ali and his descendants being secured in the Government of that Province in the same way that a former Pasha of Scutari and his family were so secured; the Pasha continuing to be the vassal of the Porte, paying a reasonable tribute, furnishing a contingent of men, and being bound like any other Pasha by the treaties which his sovereign might make. Such an arrangement would appear to be equitable between the parties, because, on the one hand, it would secure the Sultan against many dangers and inconveniences which arise from the present occupation of Syria by the Pasha; while, on the other hand, it would afford to the Pasha that security as to the future fate of his family, his anxiety about which, he has often declared to be the main cause of his desire to obtain some final and permanent arrangement.

It appears to Her Majesty's Government that if the Five Powers were to agree upon such a plan, and were to propose it to the two parties, with all the authority which belongs to the Great Powers of Europe, such an arrangement would be carried into effect, and through its means, Europe would be delivered from a great and imminent danger.

Parliamentary Papers, 1841, xxix, pp. 117–19.

DOCUMENT 13 **METTERNICH ON THE PROBABLE CONSEQUENCES OF AN OTTOMAN COLLAPSE**

Metternich predicted the consequences of an Ottoman collapse in a circular of 11 October 1840.

The day the Sultan's throne collapses, the empire itself will break up into several parts, some of which will pass into the hands of Christian Powers while others will endeavour to set themselves up as more or less independent States, offering the unedifying spectacle of Moslem anarchy such as characterized the regencies in Africa for centuries. A vast expanse of land will become the empire of the desert and remain under the rule of nomadic hordes ... As for Europe, her fate when this heavy blow falls will be wars of political rivalry.

G. de Bertier de Sauvigny, *Metternich and His Times*, Darton, Longman and Todd, 1962, p. 248.

DOCUMENT 14 **A RUSSIAN MEMORANDUM REGARDING A POSSIBLE ANGLO-RUSSIAN JOINT POLICY TOWARDS THE OTTOMAN EMPIRE, 1844**

The memorandum was composed by Count von Nesselrode, the Russian Foreign Minister, following Tsar Nicholas's visit to England in June 1844.

Russia and England are mutually penetrated with the conviction that it is for their common interest that the Ottoman Porte should maintain itself in the state of independence and of territorial possession which at present constitutes that Empire, as that political combination is the one which is most compatible with the general interest of the maintenance of peace.

Being agreed on this principle, Russia and England have an equal interest in uniting their efforts in order to keep up the existence of the Ottoman Empire, and to avert all the dangers which can place in jeopardy its safety.

With this object the essential point is to suffer the Porte to live in repose, without needlessly disturbing it by diplomatic bickerings, and without interfering without absolute necessity in its internal affairs.

In order to carry out skilfully this system of forbearance, with a view to the well-understood interest of the Porte, two things must not be lost sight of. They are these:

In the first place, the Porte has a constant tendency to extricate itself from the engagements imposed upon it by the Treaties which it has concluded with other Powers. It hopes to do so with impunity, because it reckons on the mutual jealousy of the Cabinets. It thinks that if it fails in its engagements towards one of them, the rest will espouse its quarrel, and will screen it from all responsibility.

It is essential not to confirm the Porte in this delusion. Every time that it fails in its obligations towards one of the Great Powers, it is the interest of all the rest to make it sensible of its error, and seriously to exhort it to act rightly towards the Cabinet which demands just reparation.

As soon as the Porte shall perceive that it is not supported by the other Cabinets, it will give way, and the differences which have arisen will be arranged in a conciliatory manner, without any conflict resulting from them.

There is a second cause of complication which is inherent in the situation of the Porte; it is the difficulty which exists in reconciling the respect due to the sovereign authority of the Sultan, founded on the Mussulman law, with the forbearance required by the interests of the Christian population of that Empire.

This difficulty is real. In the present state of feeling in Europe the Cabinets cannot see with indifference the Christian populations in Turkey exposed to flagrant acts of oppression and religious intolerance.

It is necessary constantly to make the Ottoman Ministers sensible of this truth, and to persuade them that they can only reckon on the friendship and on the support of the Great Powers on the condition that they treat the Christian subjects of the Porte with toleration and with mildness.

While insisting on this truth it will be the duty of the foreign Representatives, on the other hand, to exert all their influence to maintain the Christian subjects of the Porte in submission to the sovereign authority.

It will be the duty of the foreign Representatives, guided by these principles, to act among themselves in a perfect spirit of agreement. If they address remonstrances to the Porte, those remonstrances must bear a real character of unanimity, though divested of one of exclusive dictation.

By persevering in this system with calmness and moderation, the Representatives of the great Cabinets of Europe will have the best chance of succeeding in the steps which they may take, without giving occasion for complications which might affect the tranquillity of the Ottoman Empire. If all the Great Powers frankly adopt this line of conduct, they will have a well-founded expectation of preserving the existence of Turkey.

However, they must not conceal from themselves how many elements of dissolution that Empire contains within itself. Unforeseen circumstances may hasten its fall, without its being in the power of the friendly Cabinets to prevent it.

As it is not given to human foresight to settle beforehand a plan of action for such or such unlooked-for case, it would be premature to discuss eventualities which may never be realised.

In the uncertainty which hovers over the future, a single fundamental idea seems to admit of a really practical application; it is that the danger which may result from a catastrophe in Turkey will be much diminished, if, in the event of its occurring, Russia and England have come to an understanding as to the course to be taken by them in common.

That understanding will be the more beneficial, inasmuch as it will have the full assent of Austria. Between her and Russia there exists already an entire conformity of principles in regard to the affairs of Turkey, in a common interest of conservatism and of peace.

In order to render their union more efficacious, there would remain nothing to be desired but that England should be seen to associate herself thereto with the same view.

The reason which recommends the establishment of this agreement is very simple.

On land Russia exercises in regard to Turkey a preponderant action.

On sea England occupies the same position.

Isolated, the action of these two Powers might do much mischief. United, it can produce a real benefit: thence, the advantage of coming to a previous understanding before having recourse to action.

This notion was in principle agreed upon during the Emperor's last residence in London. The result was the eventual engagement, that if anything unforeseen occurred in Turkey, Russia and England should previously concert together as to the course which they should pursue in common.

The object for which Russia and England will have to come to an understanding may be expressed in the following manner:

1. To seek to maintain the existence of the Ottoman Empire in its present state, so long as that political combination shall be possible.

2. If we foresee that it must crumble to pieces, to enter into previous concert as to everything relating to the establishment of a new order of things, intended to replace that which now exists, and in conjunction with each other to see that the change which may have occurred in the internal situation of that Empire shall not injuriously affect either the security of their own States and the rights which the Treaties assure to them respectively, or the maintenance of the balance of power in Europe.

For the purpose thus stated, the policy of Russia and of Austria, as we have already said, is closely united by the principle of perfect identity. If England, as the principal Maritime Power, acts in concert with them, it is to be supposed that France will find herself obliged to act in conformity with the course agreed upon between St. Petersburgh, London, and Vienna.

Conflict between the Great Powers being thus obviated, it is to be hoped that the peace of Europe will be maintained even in the midst of such serious circumstances. It is to secure this object of common interest, if the case occurs, that, as the Emperor agreed with Her Britannic Majesty's Ministers during his residence in England, the previous understanding which Russia and England shall establish between themselves must be directed.

Parliamentary Papers, 1854, vol. 71, part 6.

DOCUMENT 15   CONVERSATIONS BETWEEN TSAR
NICHOLAS I AND SIR GEORGE HAMILTON
SEYMOUR, THE BRITISH MINISTER TO
RUSSIA, JANUARY – FEBRUARY 1853

*When these conversations were held, relations between France and Russia
were deteriorating rapidly.*

1. SEYMOUR TO LORD RUSSELL, 22 JANUARY 1853

On the 14th instant, in consequence of a summons which I received from
the Chancellor, I waited upon the Emperor, and had the honour of holding
with His Imperial Majesty the very interesting conversation of which it will
be my duty to offer your Lordship an account, which, if imperfect, will, at
all events, not be incorrect.

I found His Majesty alone; he received me with great kindness, saying,
that I had appeared desirous to speak to him upon Eastern affairs; that, on
his side, there was no indisposition to do so, but that he must begin at a
remote period.

You know, His Majesty said, the dreams and plans in which the Empress
Catherine was in the habit of indulging; these were handed down to our
time; but while I inherited immense territorial possessions, I did not inherit
those visions, those intentions if you like to call them so. On the contrary,
my country is so vast, so happily circumstanced in every way, that it would
be unreasonable in me to desire more territory or more power than I
possess; on the contrary, I am the first to tell you that our great, perhaps
our only danger, is that which would arise from an extension given to an
Empire already too large.

Close to us lies Turkey, and in our present condition, nothing better for
our interests can be desired; the times have gone by when we had anything
to fear from the fanatical spirit or the military enterprise of the Turks, and
yet the country is strong enough, or has hitherto been strong enough, to
preserve its independence, and to insure respectful treatment from other
countries.

Well, in that Empire there are several millions of Christians whose
interests I am called upon to watch over (*surveiller*), while the right of doing
so is secured to me by Treaty. I may truly say that I make a moderate and
sparing use of my right, and I will freely confess that it is one which is
attended with obligations occasionally very inconvenient; but I cannot
recede from the discharge of a distinct duty. Our religion, as established in
this country, came to us from the East, and there are feelings, as well as
obligations, which never must be lost sight of.

Now Turkey, in the condition which I have described, has by degrees
fallen into such a state of decrepitude that, as I told you the other night,
eager as we all are for the prolonged existence of the man (and that I am as
desirous as you can be for the continuance of his life, I beg you to believe),
he may suddenly die upon our hands (*nous rester sur les bras*); we cannot

resuscitate what is dead; if the Turkish Empire falls, it falls to rise no more; and I put it to you, therefore, whether it is not better to be provided beforehand for a contingency, than to incur the chaos, confusion, and the certainty of an European war, all of which must attend the catastrophe if it should occur unexpectedly, and before some ulterior system has been sketched; this is the point to which I am desirous that you should call the attention of your Government.

Sir, I replied, your Majesty is so frank with me, that I am sure you will have the goodness to permit me to speak with the same openness. I would then observe, that deplorable as is the condition of Turkey, it is a country which has long been plunged in difficulties supposed by many to be insurmountable.

With regard to contingent arrangements, Her Majesty's Government, as your Majesty is well aware, objects, as a general rule, to taking engagements upon possible eventualities, and would, perhaps, be particularly disinclined to doing so in this instance. If I may be allowed to say so, a great disinclination (répugnance) might be expected in England, to disposing by anticipation (d'escompter) of the succession of an old friend and ally.

The rule is a good one, the Emperor replied, good at all times, especially in times of uncertainty and change, like the present; still it is of the greatest importance that we should understand one another, and not allow events to take us by surprise; "Now I desire to speak to you as a friend and as a *gentleman*; if England and I arrive at an understanding of this matter, as regards the rest, it matters little to me; it is indifferent to me what others do or think. Frankly then, I tell you plainly, that if England thinks of establishing herself one of these days at Constantinople, I will not allow it. I do not attribute this intention to you, but it is better on these occasions to speak plainly; for my part, I am equally disposed to take the engagement not to establish myself there, as proprietor that is to say, for as occupier I do not say: it might happen that circumstances, if no previous provision were made, if everything should be left to chance, might place me in the position of occupying Constantinople."

I thanked His Majesty for the frankness of his declarations. and for the desire which he had expressed of acting cordially and openly with Her Majesty's Government, observing at the same time, that such an understanding appeared the best security against the sudden danger to which His Majesty had alluded. I added that, although unprepared to give a decided opinion upon questions of such magnitude and delicacy, it appeared to me possible that some such arrangement might be made between Her Majesty's Government and His Majesty, as might guard, if not for, at least against, certain contingencies.

To render my meaning more clear I said further: I can only repeat, Sir, that in my opinion, Her Majesty's Government will be indisposed to make certain arrangements connected with the downfall of Turkey, but it is possible that they may be ready to pledge themselves against certain arrangements which might, in that event, be attempted.

His Imperial Majesty then alluded to a conversation which he had held, the last time he was in England, with the Duke of Wellington, and to the motives which had compelled him to open himself to his Grace; then, as now, His Majesty was, he said, eager to provide against events which, in the absence of any concert, might compel him to act in a manner opposed to the views of Her Majesty's Government.

The conversation passed to the events of the day, when the Emperor briefly recapitulated his claims upon the Holy Places, claims recognised by the Firman of last February, and confirmed by a sanction to which His Majesty said he attached much more importance—the word of a Sovereign.

The execution of promises so made, and so ratified, the Emperor said he must insist upon, but was willing to believe that his object would be attained by negotiation, the last advices from Constantinople being rather more satisfactory.

I expressed my belief that negotiation, followed, as I supposed it had been, by the threats of military measures, would be found sufficient to secure a compliance with the just demands of Russia. I added, that I desired to state to His Majesty what I had previously read from a written paper to his Minister, viz., that what I feared for Turkey were not the intentions of His Majesty, but the actual result of the measures which appeared to be in contemplation. That I would repeat, that two consequences might be anticipated from the appearance of an Imperial army on the frontiers of Turkey—the one the counter-demonstration which might be provoked on the part of France; the other, and the more serious, the rising, on the part of the Christian population, against the Sultan's authority, already so much weakened by revolts, and by a severe financial crisis.

The Emperor assured me that no movement of his forces had yet taken place (n'ont pas bougé), and expressed his hope that no advance would be required.

With regard to a French expedition to the Sultan's dominions. His Majesty intimated that such a step would bring affairs to an immediate crisis; that a sense of honour would compel him to send his forces into Turkey without delay or hesitation; that if the result of such an advance should prove to be the overthrow of the Great Turk (le Grand Turc), he should regret the event, but should feel that he had acted as he was compelled to do.

To the above report I have only, I think, to add, that the Emperor desired to leave it to my discretion to communicate or not to his Minister the particulars of our conversation; and that before I left the room, His Imperial Majesty said, You will report what has passed between us to the Queen's Government, and you will say that I shall be ready to receive any communication which it may be their wish to make to me upon the subject.

The other topics touched upon by the Emperor are mentioned in another despatch. With regard to the extremely important overture to which this report relates, I will only observe, that as it is my duty to record impressions, as well as facts and statements, I am bound to say, that if words, tone, and manner offer any criterion by which intentions are to be judged, the Emperor is prepared to act with perfect fairness and openness towards Her Majesty's Government. His Majesty has, no doubt, his own objects in view; and he is, in my opinion, too strong a believer in the imminence of dangers in Turkey. I am, however, impressed with the belief, that in carrying out those objects, as in guarding against those dangers, His Majesty is sincerely desirous of acting in harmony with Her Majesty's Government.

I would now submit to your Lordship that this overture cannot with propriety pass unnoticed by Her Majesty's Government.

It has been on a first occasion glanced at, and on a second distinctly made by the Emperor himself to the Queen's Minister at his Court, whilst the conversation held some years ago with the Duke of Wellington proves that the object in view is one which has long occupied the thoughts of His Imperial Majesty.

If, then, the proposal were to remain unanswered, a decided advantage would be secured to the Imperial Cabinet, which, in the event of some great catastrophe taking place in Turkey, would be able to point to proposals made to England, and which, not having been responded to, left the Emperor at liberty, or placed him under the necessity, of following his own line of policy in the East.

Again, I would remark that the anxiety expressed by the Emperor, even looking to his own interests, for an extension of the days "of the dying man," appears to me to justify Her Majesty's Government in proposing to His Imperial Majesty to unite with England in the adoption of such measures as may lead to prop up the falling authority of the Sultan.

Lastly, I would observe that even if the Emperor should be found disinclined to lend himself to such a course of policy as might arrest the downfall of Turkey, his declarations to me pledge him to be ready to take beforehand, in concert with Her Majesty's Government, such precautions as may possibly prevent the fatal crisis being followed by a scramble for the rich inheritance which would remain to be disposed of.

A noble triumph would be obtained by the civilization of the nineteenth century, if the void left by the extinction of Mahommedan rule in Europe could be filled up without an interruption of the general peace, in consequence of the precautions adopted by the two principal Governments the most interested in the destinies of Turkey.

2. LORD RUSSELL TO SEYMOUR, 9 FEBRUARY 1853

I have received, and laid before the Queen, your secret and confidential despatch of the 22nd of January.

Her Majesty, upon this as upon former occasions, is happy to acknowledge the moderation, the frankness. and the friendly disposition of His Imperial Majesty.

Her Majesty has directed me to reply in the same spirit of temperate, candid, and amicable discussion.

The question raised by His Imperial Majesty is a very serious one. It is, supposing the contingency of the dissolution of the Turkish Empire to be probable, or even imminent, whether it is not better to be provided beforehand for a contingency, than to incur the chaos, confusion, and the certainty of an European war, all of which must attend the catastrophe if it should occur unexpectedly, and before some ulterior system has been sketched; this is the point, said His Imperial Majesty, to which I am desirous that you should call the attention of your Government.

In considering this grave question, the first reflection which occurs to Her Majesty's Government is that no actual crisis has occurred which renders necessary a solution of this vast European problem. Disputes have arisen respecting the Holy Places, but these are without the sphere of the internal government of Turkey, and concern Russia and France rather than the Sublime Porte. Some disturbance of the relations between Austria and the Porte has been caused by the Turkish attack on Montenegro; but this, again, relates rather to dangers affecting the frontier of Austria than the authority and safety of the Sultan; so that there is no sufficient cause for intimating to the Sultan that he cannot keep peace at home, or preserve friendly relations with his neighbours.

It occurs further to Her Majesty's Government to remark, that the event which is contemplated is not definitely fixed in point of time. When William the Third and Louis the Fourteenth disposed, by treaty, of the succession of Charles the Second of Spain, they were providing for an event which could not be far off. The infirmities of the Sovereign of Spain, and the certain end of any human life, made the contingency in prospect both sure and near. The death of the Spanish King was in no way hastened by the Treaty of Partition. The same thing may be said of the provision, made in the last century, for the disposal of Tuscany upon the decease of the last prince of the house of Medici. But the contingency of the dissolution of the Ottoman Empire is of another kind. It may happen twenty, fifty, or a hundred years hence.

In these circumstances it would hardly be consistent with the friendly feelings towards the Sultan which animate the Emperor of Russia, no less than the Queen of Great Britain, to dispose beforehand of the provinces under his dominion. Besides this consideration, however, it must be observed, that an agreement made in such a case tends very surely to hasten the contingency for which it is intended to provide. Austria and France could not, in fairness, be kept in ignorance of the transaction, nor would such concealment be consistent with the end of preventing a European war. Indeed, such concealment cannot be intended by His Imperial Majesty. It is to be inferred that, as soon as Great Britain and Russia should have agreed on the course to be pursued, and have determined to enforce it, they should communicate their intentions to the Great Powers of Europe. An agreement thus made, and thus communicated, would not be very long a secret; and while it would alarm and alienate the Sultan, the knowledge of its existence would stimulate all his enemies to increased violence and more obstinate conflict. They would fight with the conviction that they must ultimately triumph; while the Sultan's generals and troops would feel that no immediate success could save their cause from final overthrow. Thus would be produced and strengthened that very anarchy which is now feared, and the foresight of the friends of the patient would prove the cause of his death.

Her Majesty's Government need scarcely enlarge on the dangers attendant on the execution of any similar Convention. The example of the Succession War is enough to show how little such agreements are respected when a pressing temptation urges their violation. The position of the Emperor of Russia as depositary, but not proprietor, of Constantinople, would be exposed to numberless hazards, both from the long-cherished ambition of his own nation, and the jealousies of Europe. The ultimate proprietor, whoever he might be, would hardly be satisfied with the inert, supine attitude of the heirs of Mahomet the Second. A great influence on the affairs of Europe seems naturally to belong to the Sovereign of Constantinople, holding the gates of the Mediterranean and the Black Sea.

That influence might be used in favour of Russia; it might be used to control and curb her power.

His Imperial Majesty has justly and wisely said: My country is so vast, so happily circumstanced in every way, that it would be unreasonable in me to desire more territory or more power than I possess. On the contrary, he observed, our great, perhaps our only danger, is that which would arise from an extension given to an Empire already too large. A vigorous and ambitious State, replacing the Sublime Porte, might, however, render war on the part of Russia a necessity for the Emperor or his successors.

Thus European conflict would arise from the very means taken to prevent it; for neither England nor France, nor probably Austria would be content to see Constantinople permanently in the hands of Russia.

On the part of Great Britain, Her Majesty's Government at once declare that they renounce all intention or wish to hold Constantinople. His Imperial Majesty may be quite secure upon this head. They are likewise ready to give an assurance that they will enter into no agreement to provide for the contingency of the fall of Turkey without previous communication with the Emperor of Russia.

Upon the whole, then, Her Majesty's Government are persuaded that no course of policy can be adopted more wise, more disinterested, more beneficial to Europe than that which His Imperial Majesty has so long followed, and which will render his name more illustrious than that of the most famous Sovereigns who have sought immortality by unprovoked conquest and ephemeral glory.

With a view to the success of this policy it is desirable that the utmost forbearance should be manifested towards Turkey; that any demands which the Great Powers of Europe may have to make, should be made matter of friendly negotiation rather than of peremptory demand; that military and naval demonstrations to coerce the Sultan should as much as possible be avoided; that differences with respect to matters affecting Turkey, within the competence of the Sublime Porte, should be decided after mutual concert between the Great Powers, and not be forced upon the weakness of the Turkish Government.

To these cautions Her Majesty's Government wish to add, that in their view it is essential that the Sultan should be advised to treat his Christian subjects in conformity with the principles of equity and religious freedom which prevail generally among the enlightened nations of Europe. The more the Turkish Government adopts the rules of impartial law and equal administration, the less will the Emperor of Russia find it necessary to apply that exceptional protection which His Imperial Majesty has found so burthensome and inconvenient, though no doubt prescribed by duty and sanctioned by Treaty.

You may read this despatch to Count Nesselrode, and, if it is desired, you may yourself place a copy of it in the hands of the Emperor. In that case you will accompany its presentation with those assurances of friendship and confidence on the part of Her Majesty the Queen, which the conduct of His Imperial Majesty was so sure to inspire.

3. SEYMOUR TO LORD RUSSELL, 21 FEBRUARY 1853

The Emperor came up to me last night, at a party of the Grand Duchess Hereditary's, and in the most gracious manner took me apart, saying that he desired to speak to me. After expressing, in flattering terms, the confidence which he has in me, and his readiness to speak to me without reserve upon matters of the greatest moment, as, His Majesty observed, he had proved in a late conversation, he said: And it is well it is so: for what I most desire is, that there should be the greatest intimacy between the two Governments: it never was so necessary as at present. Well, the Emperor continued, so you have got your answer, and you are to bring it to me to-morrow?

I am to have that honour, Sir, I answered; but your Majesty is aware that the nature of the reply is very exactly what I had led you to expect.

So I was sorry to hear; but I think your Government does not well understand my object. I am not so eager about what shall be done when the bear dies, as I am to determine with England what shall not be done upon that event taking place.

But, Sir, I replied, allow me to observe, that we have no reason to think that the Bear (to use your Majesty's expression) is dying. We are as much interested as we believe your Majesty to be in his continuing to live; while for myself, I will venture to remark that experience shows me that countries do not die in such a hurry:– I have seen by our Archives both in Turkey and Portugal that these two countries have for years past been considered in a perishing state, and yet there they remain, and there Turkey will remain for many a year, unless some unforeseen crisis should occur. It is precisely, Sir, for the avoidance of all circumstances likely to produce such a crisis, that Her Majesty's Government reckons upon your generous assistance.

Then, rejoined the Emperor, I will tell you, that if your Government has been led to believe that Turkey retains any elements of existence, your Government must have received incorrect information. I repeat to you that the Bear is dying, you may give him musk, but even musk will not long keep him alive, and we can never allow such an event to take us by surprise. We must come to some understanding; and this we should do, I am convinced, if I could hold but ten minutes' conversation with your Ministers—with Lord Aberdeen, for instance, who knows me so well, who has full confidence in me, as I have in him. And remember, I do not ask for a Treaty or a Protocol; a general understanding is all I require—that between gentlemen is sufficient; and in this case I am certain that the confidence would be as great on the side of the Queen's Ministers as on mine. So no more for the present; you will come to me to-morrow, and you will remember that as often as you think your conversing with me will promote a good understanding upon any point, you will send word that you wish to see me.

I thanked His Majesty very cordially, adding that I could assure him that Her Majesty's Government, I was convinced, considered his word, once given, as good as a bond.

It is hardly necessary that I should observe to your Lordship, that this short conversation, briefly but correctly reported, offers matter for most anxious reflection.

It can hardly be otherwise but that the Sovereign who insists with such pertinacity upon the impending fall of a neighbouring State, must have settled in his own mind that the hour, if not of its dissolution, at all events for its dissolution, must be at hand.

I will only remark to your Lordship, as a point of evidence which goes far towards establishing a settled purpose, that the expression of Musk being insufficient to keep alive the sinking Turk was used to me ten days ago by one of the Emperor's most confidential Servants.

Then, as now, I reflected that this assumption would hardly be ventured upon unless some, perhaps general, but at all events intimate, understanding, existed between Russia and Austria.

Supposing my suspicion to be well founded, the Emperor's object is to engage Her Majesty's Government, in conjunction with his own Cabinet and that of Vienna, in some scheme for the ultimate partition of Turkey, and for the exclusion of France from the arrangement.

Parliamentary Papers, 1854, vol. 71, part 5

DOCUMENT 16   NICHOLAS I ON RUSSIAN POLICY IN THE
NEAR EAST, 1853

*Nicholas I noted his thoughts on Russian policy in the Near East, shortly
before Menshikov's departure for Constantinople in February 1853.*

What should be our objective?
1. Reparation.
2. Guarantees for the future. What form can they take?
3. Conservation of the position as it used to be. Is this probable?

What are the means of attaining our objective?
1. Negotiations:
    a) by letter
    b) by the sending of an embassy. Advantages and drawbacks.
2. Intimidation by recall of our mission. Drawbacks.
3. By force:
    a) declaration of war. Drawbacks;
    b) surprise by occupation of the principalities. Drawbacks;
    c) surprise attack on Constantinople. Advantages, drawbacks; chances of success.

Probable results:
1. Turkey will give way.
2. She will not give way; destruction of Constantinople.
3. The defeated Turkish army retreats towards Gallipoli or Enos.
4. Occupation of the Dardanelles.
5. The French send a fleet and an expeditionary force. Conflicts with them.

Chances of success; possibility of setbacks:
6. We have the upper hand, Constantinople and the Dardanelles are in our hands, the Turkish army is routed.
7. Fall of the Ottoman Empire.
8. Should we reestablish it and on what conditions?
9. Can we reestablish it with a chance of success?
10. With what should it be replaced?
    a) Keep all its European territory. Impossible.
    b) Keep Constantinople and the Dardanelles – disadvantages.
    c) Constantinople alone – an impossibility.
    d) Division into independent provinces.
    e) Reestablishment of the Byzantine Empire.
    f) Reunion with Greece.
       Impossibility of both.
    g) Division between ourselves, Austria, England and France.
    h) What to do with Constantinople.
    i) The least bad of all bad solutions.
    a) The Principalities and Bulgaria as far as Kistendji to Russia.
    b) Serbia and Bulgaria independent.

c) The coasts of the Archipelago and the Adriatic to Austria.

d) Egypt to England: perhaps Cyprus and Rhodes.

e) Crete to France.

f) The islands of the Archipelago to Greece.

g) Constantinople a free city; the Bosphorus Russian garrison; the Dardanelles Austrian garrison.

h) Complete freedom of trade.

i) The Turkish Empire in Asia Minor.

Anderson, [4], pp. 68–9.

DOCUMENT 17   **THE BRITISH DECLARATION OF WAR, 28 MARCH 1854**

The declaration sets out in some detail the British view of the dispute.

It is with deep Regret that Her Majesty announces the Failure of Her anxious and protracted Endeavours to preserve for Her People and for Europe the Blessings of Peace.

The unprovoked Aggression of the Emperor of Russia against the Sublime Porte has been persisted in with such Disregard of Consequences, that after the Rejection by the Emperor of Russia of Terms which the Emperor of Austria, the Emperor of the French, and the King of Prussia, as well as Her Majesty, considered just and equitable, Her Majesty is compelled, by a Sense of what is due to the Honour of Her Crown, to the Interests of Her People, and to the Independence of the States of Europe, to come forward in defence of an Ally whose Territory is invaded and whose Dignity and Independence are assailed.

Her Majesty, in justification of the Course She is about to pursue, refers to the Transactions in which Her Majesty has been engaged.

The Emperor of Russia had some Cause of Complaint against the Sultan with reference to the Settlement, which His Highness had sanctioned, of the conflicting Claims of the Greek and Latin Churches to a Portion of the Holy Places of Jerusalem and its Neighbourhood. To the Complaint of the Emperor of Russia on this Head Justice was done; and Her Majesty's Ambassador at Constantinople had the Satisfaction of promoting an Arrangement to which no Exception was taken by the Russian Government.

But while the Russian Government repeatedly assured the Government of Her Majesty that the Mission of Prince Menchikoff to Constantinople was exclusively directed to the Settlement of the Question of the Holy Places at Jerusalem, Prince Menchikoff himself pressed upon the Porte other Demands of a far more serious and important Character, the Nature of which he in the first instance endeavoured, as far as possible, to conceal from Her Majesty's Ambassador. And these Demands, thus studiously concealed, affected not the Privileges of the Greek Church at Jerusalem, but the Position of many Millions of Turkish Subjects in their Relations to their Sovereign the Sultan.

These Demands were rejected by the spontaneous Decision of the Sublime Porte.

Two Assurances had been given to Her Majesty; One, that the Mission of Prince Menchikoff only regarded the Holy Places; the other, that his Mission would be of a conciliatory Character.

In both respects Her Majesty's just Expectations were disappointed.

Demands were made, which, in the Opinion of the Sultan, extended to the Substitution of the Emperor of Russia's Authority for his own, over a large Portion of his Subjects; and those Demands were enforced by a Threat; and when Her Majesty learnt that, on announcing the Termination of his Mission, Prince Menchikoff declared that the Refusal of his Demands would impose upon the Imperial Government the Necessity of seeking a Guarantee by its own Power, Her Majesty thought proper that Her Fleet should leave Malta, and, in co-operation with that of His Majesty the Emperor of the French, take up its Station in the Neighbourhood of the Dardanelles.

So long as the Negotiation bore an amicable Character, Her Majesty refrained from any Demonstration of Force. But when, in addition to the Assemblage of large Military Forces on the Frontier of Turkey, the Ambassador of Russia intimated that serious Consequences would ensue from the Refusal of the Sultan to comply with unwarrantable Demands, Her Majesty deemed it right, in conjunction with the Emperor of the French, to give an unquestionable Proof of Her Determination to support the Sovereign Rights of the Sultan.

The Russian Government has maintained that the Determination of the Emperor to occupy the Principalities was taken in consequence of the Advance of the Fleets of England and France. But the Menace of Invasion of the Turkish Territory was conveyed in Count Nesselrode's Note to Rechid Pacha, of the 19/31 May, and re-stated in his Despatch to Baron Brunnow, of the 20 May/1 June which announced the Determination of the Emperor of Russia to order his Troops to occupy the Principalities, if the Porte did not within a Week comply with the Demands of Russia.

The Despatch to Her Majesty's Ambassador, at Constantinople, authorizing him in certain specified Contingencies to send for the British Fleet, was dated the 31st May, and the Order sent direct from England to Her Majesty's Admiral to proceed to the Neighbourhood of the Dardanelles, was dated the 2nd of June.

The Determination to occupy the Principalities was therefore taken before the Orders for the Advance of the combined Squadrons were given ...

... The Time has, however, now arrived when the Advice and Remonstrances of the Four Powers having proved wholly ineffectual, and the Military Preparations of Russia becoming daily more extended, it is but too obvious that the Emperor of Russia has entered upon a Course of

Policy which, if unchecked, must lead to the Destruction of the Ottoman Empire.

In this Conjuncture, Her Majesty feels called upon by Regard for an Ally, the Integrity and Independence of whose Empire have been recognized as essential to the Peace of Europe, by the Sympathies of Her People with Right against Wrong, by a Desire to avert from Her Dominions most injurious Consequences, and to save Europe from the Preponderance of a Power which has violated the Faith of Treaties, and defies the Opinion of the civilized World, to take up Arms, in conjunction with the Emperor of the French, for the Defence of the Sultan.

Public Record Office, London, ADM 116/3239.

DOCUMENT 18   THE TREATY OF PARIS, 30 MARCH 1856

The 'firman' referred to in Article IX is the Hatt-i Humayun (Imperial Rescript) of 18 February 1856, which promised protection for the life, honour, and property of the Sultan's subjects.

Article VII. Her Majesty the Queen of the United Kingdom of Great Britain and Ireland, His Majesty the Emperor of Austria, His Majesty the Emperor of the French, His Majesty the King of Prussia, His Majesty the Emperor of all the Russias, and His Majesty the King of Sardinia declare the Sublime Porte admitted to participate in the advantages of the public law and system (*concert*) of Europe. Their Majesties engage, each on his part, to respect the independence and the territorial integrity of the Ottoman Empire; guarantee in common the strict observance of that engagement; and will, in consequence, consider any act tending to its violation as a question of general interest.

Article VIII. If there should arise between the Sublime Porte and one or more of the other signing Powers, any misunderstanding which might endanger the maintenance of their relations, the Sublime Porte, and each of such Powers, before having recourse to the use of force, shall afford the other Contracting Parties the opportunity of preventing such an extremity by means of their mediation.

Article IX. His Imperial Majesty the Sultan, having, in his constant solicitude for the welfare of his subjects, issued a firman which, while ameliorating their condition without distinction of religion or of race, records his generous intentions towards the Christian population of his Empire, and wishing to give a further proof of his sentiments in that respect, has resolved to communicate to the Contracting Parties the said firman, emanating spontaneously from his sovereign will.

The Contracting Parties recognize the high value of this communication. It is clearly understood that it cannot, in any ease, give to the said Powers the right to interfere, either collectively or separately, in the relations of His Majesty the Sultan with his subjects, nor in the internal administration of his Empire.

Article X. The Convention of the 13th of July, 1841, which maintains the ancient rule of the Ottoman Empire relative to the closing of the Straits of the Bosphorus and of the Dardanelles, has been revised by common consent.

The Act concluded for that purpose, and in conformity with that principle, between the High Contracting Parties, is and remains annexed to the present Treaty, and shall have the same force and validity as if it formed an integral part thereof.

Article XI. The Black Sea is neutralized: its waters and its ports, thrown open to the mercantile marine of every nation, are formally and in perpetuity interdicted to the flag of war, either of the Powers possessing its coasts, or of any other Power, with the exceptions mentioned in Articles XIV and XIX of the present Treaty ...

Article XIII. The Black Sea being neutralized according to the terms of Article XI, the maintenance or establishment upon its coasts of military-maritime arsenals becomes alike unnecessary and purposeless; in consequence, His Majesty the Emperor of all the Russias, and His Imperial Majesty the Sultan engage not to establish or to maintain upon that coast any military-maritime arsenal ...

Article XX. In exchange for the towns, ports, and territories enumerated in Article IV of the present Treaty, and in order more fully to secure the freedom of the navigation of the Danube, His Majesty the Emperor of all the Russias consents to the rectification of his frontier in Bessarabia.

Parliamentary Papers, 1856, lxi, pp. 21–7.

DOCUMENT 19   NAPOLEON III ON FRENCH POLICY REGARDING SYRIA AND THE LEBANON, 1860

Napoleon III explained his attitude to the Syrian crisis in a letter to Victor Persigny, the French Ambassador in London, on 29 July 1860.

When La Valette left for Constantinople the instructions which I gave him amounted to this: 'Bend every effort to maintain the *status quo*; it is to the interest of France that Turkey live as long as possible.'

Now come the massacres in Syria and they say that I am quite happy to have found an occasion for making a small war or for playing a new role. The truth is that this credits me with precious little common sense. If I immediately proposed an expedition it was because my feelings are those of the people who have placed me at its head and because the news from Syria filled me· with indignation. Nevertheless my first thought was to reach an understanding with England.

What interest other than that of humanity would prompt me to send troops into this country? ... I said it in 1852 at Bordeaux and it remains my opinion today – I have great conquests to make, but in France ...

I would very much prefer not to be obliged to make a Syrian expedition, and in any case not to make it alone, first because it will constitute a great expense, and second because I am afraid that this intervention will precipitate the Eastern Question, but, on the other hand, I cannot see how to resist the public opinion of my country, which will never understand the failure to punish not only the murder of Christians but also the burning of our consulates, the mutilation of our flag, and the pillaging of monasteries entrusted to our protection.

Archives Diplomatiques, Paris, 1861 ff i, pp. 98–100.

DOCUMENT 20   **AN AUSTRIAN ACCOUNT OF THE REICHSTADT AGREEMENT, 8 JULY 1876**

Following the meeting of Andrassy and Gorchakov at Reichstadt, different versions of the agreement were drawn up. In the Russian version it was assumed that, in the event of a Turkish defeat, Serbia would annex parts of Old Serbia and Bosnia, while Montenegro would acquire the whole of Herzegovina. In the Austrian version, which is given below, it was assumed that Austria–Hungary would annex the greater part of both Bosnia and Herzegovina.

The reasoning has been on two hypotheses: That of the Turks coming out of the struggle victorious and that of their being defeated.

In the event of the first, it was agreed not to let them obtain more than certain guarantees, which should not be excessive. Efforts were to be made to prevent the war from becoming a struggle for extermination; Serbia and Montenegro were to be maintained in the territorial limits which now circumscribe these two principalities, and the idea of a reestablishment of the Turkish fortresses in Serbia was to be opposed.

In the case of Serbia, the character of an independent state was not to be recognized; but agreement was reached to recognize it in the case of Montenegro, whatever might be the interpretation which other Powers might wish to give to the political position of the Black Mountain. As a consequence of this independence, the Austro-Hungarian Government has declared itself ready to close the two ports of Klek and Cattaro to all importation of arms and of munitions for the opposing parties; although it foresees very grave objections on the part of the Turkish Government to the closing of the first of these ports.

Concerning the insurgents, it was agreed (always in the event of the victory of the Turks) to make common efforts to guarantee to them the liberties and the reforms which have been requested of the Porte and promised by it.

In all the eventualities above mentioned, there was to be no question of any territorial modification, either on one side or on the other.

In passing to the second hypothesis, that of a defeat of the Turks, the following are the ideas on which agreement was reached:

Austria-Hungary having declared that she cannot permit that Serbia occupy and keep by right of conquest the enclave comprised between Dalmatia, Croatia, and Slavonia, as this would mean a danger to the provinces of the Monarchy, especially to its Dalmatian littoral, which, extending like a thin ribbon, would evidently have to be annexed to the new Serbia or else place the Imperial and Royal Government under the necessity of annexing Serbia herself, which is excluded from the programme; it was agreed that Serbia should obtain an extension of territory in the Drina region in Bosnia, at the same time as in that of Novi-Bazar in Old Serbia and in the direction of the Lim. On her side Montenegro should be rounded out by the annexation of a part of Herzegovina adjoining her territories; she should obtain the port of Spizza as well as an aggrandizement in the region of the Lim, in such a way that the tongue of land which now stretches between Serbia and Montenegro should be divided between the two principalities by the course of this river.

The rest of Bosnia and Herzegovina should be annexed to Austria-Hungary. Russia should resume her natural frontiers of before 1856 and might round herself off in the region of the Black Sea and in Turkey in Asia to the extent that this should be necessary for the establishment of better frontiers for herself in this direction and to serve as an equivalent for the slice of territory to be annexed to Austria-Hungary.

Bulgaria, Rumelia, and Albania might form autonomous states. Thessaly and the island of Crete should be annexed to Greece.

Constantinople, with a territory to be determined, should become a free city.

It was equally agreed that all these ideas should be kept secret between the two Emperors and their respective Ministers; that they should not be communicated to the other Powers, and more particularly not to the Serbians and Montenegrins, until the moment of their realization should arrive.

A. F. Pribram, *The Secret Treaties of Austria–Hungary, 1879–1914*, Cambridge, Mass., 1920, ii, pp. 189–91.

DOCUMENT 21   BISMARCK ON A POSSIBLE FUTURE
ALIGNMENT OF THE POWERS, 1877

Bismarck set out his views on a possible future alignment of the powers in a note dictated on 15 June 1877.

I wish that, without making it too noticeable, we should encourage the English with any designs they may have on Egypt; I consider it in our interest, and useful for us in the future, to promote an arrangement between England and Russia giving the prospect of good relations between them similar to those at the beginning of the century, and shortly afterwards of both of them with us. Such a goal may not be attained, but one can never tell. If England and Russia could agree on the basis that the former would have Turkey and the latter the Black Sea, both would be in a position to be satisfied for a long time ahead with the status quo, and yet in their most important interests would be involved in a rivalry which would hardly allow them to take part in coalitions against us, quite apart from the domestic obstacles in England to such a course.

A French newspaper said of me recently that I had a 'coalition nightmare'; this kind of nightmare will long (and perhaps always) be a legitimate one for a German minister. Coalitions can be formed against us, based on the western powers with the addition of Austria, even more dangerous perhaps on a Russo-Austrian-French basis; great intimacy between two of the last-named powers would always offer the third of them a means of exerting very effective pressure on us. In our anxiety about these eventualities, I would regard as desirable results of the eastern crisis (not immediately, but in the course of years): 1. gravitation of Russian and Austrian interests and mutual rivalries towards the east; 2. Russia to be obliged to take up a strong defensive position in the East and on its coasts, and to need our alliance; 3. for England and Russia a satisfactory status quo, which would give them the same interest in keeping what they hold as we have; 4. separation of England, on account of Egypt and the Mediterranean, from France, which remains hostile to us; 5. relations between Russia and Austria which would make it difficult for them to launch against us the anti-German conspiracy to which centralist or clerical elements in Austria might be somewhat inclined.

If I were able to work, I could complete and elaborate in detail the picture I have in mind: not one of gaining territory, but of a political situation as a whole, in which all the powers except France had need of us, and would thus be deterred as far as possible from coalitions against us by their relations with each other.

The occupation of Egypt would not be sufficient in England's view to resolve the difficulties of the Dardanelles: the system of double custody, with the Dardanelles for England and the Bosphorus for Russia, is dangerous for England because in certain circumstances its fortifications at the Dardanelles could be more easily taken by land troops than defended;

that point will also have occurred to the Russians, who may perhaps be satisfied for a generation with the closing of the Black Sea. The question remains a matter for negotiation, and the whole result as I visualize it could be worked out just as easily after as before the decisive battles of this war. I would look on it as something so valuable to us as to outweigh any possible prejudicing of our Black Sea interests, leaving aside the possible safe-guarding of the latter by the treaties. Even if an Anglo-Russian war could not be averted, our goal would, in my opinion, remain the same, namely the negotiating of a peace which would satisfy both at the expense of Turkey.

W. N. Medlicott and D. K. Coveney, *Bismarck and Europe*, Edward Arnold, pp. 102–3.

DOCUMENT 22   SALISBURY ON THE ADVANTAGES OF AN ANGLO-TURKISH ALLIANCE, 1878

Salisbury set out the case for an Anglo-Turkish alliance, and a British base in the Middle East, in a letter to Sir Henry Layard, the British Ambassador in Constantinople, on 9 May 1878.

The great problem which the Turk will have to solve, as soon as he has got rid of the Russian army off his soil is – how to keep his Asiatic Empire together. Sooner or later the greater part of his European Empire *must* go. Bosnia and Bulgaria are as good as gone. We may with great efforts give him another lease of Thrace: and he may keep for a considerable time a hold on Macedonia and Albania and possible [*sic*] on Thessaly and Epirus. But he will not get soldiers from them: for the Mussulman population will tend more and more to recede: and it is from them alone that any effective army can be drawn. The European provinces may bring in money: and to some extent, and for some time, they may have a strategic value. But if the Turk is to maintain himself at Constantinople it is mainly with Asiatic soldiers that he will do it. The question is how is he to maintain himself in Asia. With the Russians at Kars, the idea of coming change will be rife over all Asia Minor – over Mesopotamia and Syria. If he has his own strength alone to trust to, no one will believe in his power of resistance. He has been beaten too often. The Arabs, and the Asiatics generally, will look to the Russian as the coming man. The Turk's only chance is to obtain the alliance of a great Power: and the only Power available is England.

Is it possible for England to give that alliance? I cannot speak yet with confidence: but I think so. For England the question of Turkey in Asia is very different from that of Turkey in Europe. The only change possible for the Asiatic Christians would be to come directly under the Government of Russia. There is and can be no question of autonomy – of young and struggling nationalities, and the rest of it. ... And, while Russian influence over the provinces of European Turkey would be a comparatively distant and indirect evil, her influence over Syria and Mesopotamia would be a very serious embarrassment, and would certainly through the connection of Baghdad with Bombay, make our hold on India more difficult. I do not, therefore, despair of England coming to the conclusion that she can undertake such a defensive alliance. But for that purpose it is, as I said before, absolutely and indispensably necessary that she should be nearer at hand than Malta.

Anderson, [4], p. 102.

DOCUMENT 23   A FRENCH COMMENT ON THE CONGRESS
OF BERLIN, 1878

W. H. Waddington, the leader of the French delegation at the Congress of Berlin, noted his impressions of the opening stages of the Congress in a letter to A. J. S. Dufaure, the French Prime Minister, on 18 June 1878.

From the day of their first meeting the Plenipotentiaries have not remained inactive. Several, when they arrived in Berlin to take part in such important negotiations, were entirely unknown to each other. Relations have been established, conversations have taken place. Each has tried to fathom the policies of those among whom he sought allies or suspected opponents. For my part I tried above all to understand the views of Austria-Hungary and England and to learn to what extent there was agreement between the two cabinets which, before the meeting of the Congress, opposed most directly the Treaty of San Stefano. It was no less interesting for us to see how one or the other, or both together, had since formed links with Russia on the essential questions upon which peace or war might depend.

The more or less calculated indiscretions of an English newspaper had not yet thrown any light on the terms of the rapprochement brought about between the government of Her Britannic Majesty and that of the Emperor Alexander, but it was already easy to see that Bulgaria had been the object of discussions and promises suitable to pave the way for a definitive entente. Without obtaining an explicit admission from Lord Beaconsfield and the Marquess of Salisbury, I have, from the first, gathered from their mouths a statement of the views of their government which conforms, in all its essentials, with the indications which today were made public. Count Andrassy, for his part, whom I saw before tackling the English plenipotentiaries, seemed to me determined to demand the setting-up of two Bulgarias, one tributary to the Porte, the other enjoying an autonomous administration but governed directly by the Sultan. Between the language of Count Andrassy and that of Lord Beaconsfield I have noticed only shades of meaning and not essential divergences which could lead to serious disagreement. Will the tributary Bulgaria, limited in the south by the Balkans, include the city of Sofia, situated in the south-west, with the adjoining territory, within her frontiers? Will the southern province, which is to be constituted under the name of Rumelia, retain Turkish garrisons or not? On these two points the Plenipotentiaries of Austria and Great Britain do not seem as yet to have taken an absolutely firm stand, but I do not see, I repeat, any reason to fear grave dissension between them when the Congress undertakes discussion of the article of the Treaty of San Stefano relating to Bulgaria.

Documents Diplomatiques Français, 1871–1914, Paris, 1930, 1st series, ii, pp. 331–3.

DOCUMENT 24   **BRITISH POLICY ON EGYPT, 1879**

On 16 October 1879 Salisbury set out his views on British policy regarding Egypt in a letter of instruction to Edward Malet, the newly-appointed British Agent and Consul-General.

As you will shortly proceed to Egypt to take up the appointment of Her Majesty's Agent and Consul-General in that country, I think it right to address to you some observations as to the principles by which your conduct should be guided.

The leading aim of our policy in Egypt is the maintenance of the neutrality of that country, that is to say, the maintenance of such a state of things that no great Power shall be more powerful there than England.

This purpose might of course be secured by the predominance of England itself, or even by the establishment of the Queen's authority in the country. Circumstances may be conceived in which this would be the only way of attaining the object; but it would not be the best method. It would not in the present state of affairs confer any other advantages than opportunities of employing English people and introducing English capital; and these would be outweighed by the responsibilities, military and financial, it would entail. The only justification of such a policy would consist in its being the only available mode of assuring the neutrality of Egypt towards us.

With this object in view it is obvious that we can have no jealousy of Native rule in itself. On the contrary, its continuance is, for us, the easiest solution of the problem. But it must not degenerate into anarchy, or perpetuate the oppression of recent years. Egypt is too much in view of the whole world, and there are too many interests attaching to it, to be suffered to relapse into the barbarous administration which in Persia and Burmah has resulted in misery so acute as to produce depopulation. An opinion would grow up in Europe in favour of intervention, which, in this case, would mean occupation; and if England could not satisfy it, she would not be able to prevent some other Power from doing so. ...

Hurewitz, [51], pp. 191–4.

DOCUMENT 25 SALISBURY ON THE CONSEQUENCES OF A RUSSIAN OCCUPATION OF CONSTANTINOPLE, 1892

Following an Admiralty report, which suggested that, in time of need, Britain might no longer be able to force the Dardanelles, Salisbury noted the implications for British policy.

The protection of Constantinople from Russian conquest has been the turning point of the policy of this country for at least forty years, and to a certain extent for forty years before that. It has been constantly assumed, both in England and abroad, that this protection of Constantinople was the special interest of Great Britain. It is our principal, if not our only, interest in the Mediterranean Sea; for if Russia were mistress of Constantinople, and of the influence which Constantinople possesses in the Levant, the route to India through the Suez Canal would be so much exposed as not to be available except in times of the profoundest peace. I need not dwell upon the effect which the Russian possession of Constantinople would have upon the Oriental mind, and upon our position in India, which is so largely dependent on prestige. But the matter of present importance is its effect upon the Mediterranean; and I cannot see, if Constantinople were no longer defensible, that any other interest in the Mediterranean is left to defend. The value of Malta, our only possession inside that sea, would at all events be diminished to an indefinite degree.

It now appears from this Report that, in the opinion of General Chapman and Captain Bridge, it is not only not possible for us to protect Constantinople, but that any effort to do so is not permissible. Even supposing the fortifications in the Dardanelles could be silenced, even supposing the Sultan asked for our presence in the Bosphorus to defend him against a Russian attack, it would yet be, in the judgement of these two officers, a step of grave peril to employ any portion of the British Mediterranean fleet in protecting him. The peril would arise, not from any danger we might incur in meeting the Russian forces, not from the strength of any fortifications the fleet would have to pass, but from the fact that this is the extreme end of the Mediterranean and that so long as the French fleet exists at Toulon, the function of the English fleet must be to remain in such a position as to prevent the French fleet at Toulon from escaping into the Atlantic and the English Channel, where it would be a grave peril to this country. They conclude, therefore, that unless we had the concurrence of France, which is of course an absurd hypothesis, or unless we had first destroyed the French fleet at Toulon, which at all events must be a very distant contingency, it is not legitimate for us to employ our fleet at the eastern end of the Mediterranean. The presence of the French fleet therefore in the harbour of Toulon, without any declaration of hostile intention or any hostile act, has the power of entirely immobilizing, and therefore neutralizing, any force that we possess or could bring under existing circumstances into the Mediterranean.

Two very grave questions arise from this strategic declaration which it must be the task of Her Majesty's Government, before any long period has elapsed, definitely to answer.

In the first place, it is a question whether any advantage arises from keeping a fleet in the Mediterranean at all. The main object of our policy is declared to be entirely out of our reach, and it is laid down that even a movement to attain it would be full of danger. There is nothing else in the Mediterranean which is worth the maintenance of so large and costly a force. If its main duty is to protect the Atlantic and the Channel, it had better go there. If it is retained in Portsmouth Harbour it will, at least, be comparatively safe from any possible attack on the part of the fleet at Toulon, and a very considerable relief will be given to the Budget of the Chancellor of the Exchequer.

Secondly, the other consideration is that our foreign policy requires to be speedily and avowedly revised. At present, it is supposed that the fall of Constantinople will be a great defeat for England. That defeat appears to be not a matter of speculation, but of absolute certainty, according to the opinion of these two distinguished officers, because we may not stir a finger to prevent it. It would surely be wise, in the interest of our own reputation, to let it be known as quickly as possible that we do not pretend to defend Constantinople, and that the protection of it from Russian attack is not, in our eyes, worthy of the sacrifices or the risks which such an effort would involve. At present, if the two officers in question are correct in their views, our policy is a policy of false pretences. If persisted in, it will involve discomfiture to all who trust in us, and infinite discredit to ourselves.

C. J. Lowe, *The Reluctant Imperialists: British Foreign Policy, 1878–1902,* Routledge and Kegan Paul, 1967, ii, pp. 86–8.

DOCUMENT 26   AEHRENTHAL'S ACCOUNT OF A
CONVERSATION WITH ISVOLSKY AT
BUCHLAU, 16 SEPTEMBER 1908

*In the memorandum of 27 August mentioned below, the Austrians had
indicated that they would respond favourably to Russian proposals
regarding the Straits, in return for Russian acceptance of an Austrian
annexation of Bosnia and Herzegovina. The Muraviev formula referred to
was an earlier agreement, which said that 'the establishment of a new order
of things in the Balkan Peninsula, outside Constantinople and the Straits,
would, in case it should occur, give rise to a special stipulation between
Austria-Hungary and Russia'.*

M. Izvolskii likewise raised the question of the political consequences of the
memorandum of 27 August, and recognised it as being in accordance with
the interests of Russia. As far as the annexation of Bosnia and Herzegovina
was concerned, M. Izvolskii tried at first to entrench himself behind the
Muraviev formula; but when I indicated that I could not be satisfied with
such an answer and that it was high time that Russia should at last take a
definitive stand on this question which had been so frequently raised, he did
not hesitate to tell me that Russia, if we should be forced to proceed to
annexation, would assume a friendly and benevolent attitude to this event.
The Russian minister at the same time recognised the great moderation and
caution expressed in our renunciation of the Sandjak [of Novibazar], which
gave reason to believe that the fait accompli of the annexation would most
probably appear in a more favourable light because of the simultaneous
withdrawal of our troops from the Sandjak.

While he was talking in general about this subject, M. Izvolskii remarked
that he did not in any way regard with mistrust the consolidation of the
territorial position of the [Habsburg] Monarchy which would be brought
about by the annexation of Bosnia and Herzegovina. However in his
consent to it he must not lose sight of the special interests of Russia, and
must also weigh the results which the modification of the Treaty of Berlin
brought about by us would have for the Balkan states and the general
position in Turkey.

As far as Russian interests were concerned, M. Izvolskii formulated the
wish which he had long cherished of a passage for Russian ships of war
through the Straits. He began with a repetition of the declaration, frequently
given by Russian statesmen on previous occasions, that Russia had no
territorial gains in view in Constantinople or its neighbourhood. In the
modification of treaty rights which he envisaged it was a matter simply of
an academic definition which should offer Russia the possibility of
strengthening her different squadrons from the reservoir of the Black Sea
fleet instead of by costly shipbuilding. In this sense it would be a matter of
our agreement for which he casually suggested the following wording:

'Austria-Hungary gives an undertaking to observe a benevolent and friendly attitude in the event of Russia seeing herself drawn by her interests to take steps to obtain free passage through the Dardanelles for individual Russian warships. It is understood that this modification of existing rights does not threaten the independence and security of the Ottoman capital and that the same facility cannot be refused to the other states with coastlines on the Black Sea.'

Anderson, [4], pp. 135–6.

DOCUMENT 27   **THE ANGLO-FRANCO-RUSSIAN AGREEMENTS OF MARCH–APRIL 1915**

France agreed to the Russian demands only after Russia had recognised Syria and Cilicia as a French sphere of influence.

(a) *Russian Circular Telegram of 4 March 1915*
The course of recent events leads His Majesty Emperor Nicholas to think that the question of Constantinople and the Straits must be definitively solved, according to the time-honoured aspirations of Russia.

Every solution will be inadequate and precarious if the city of Constantinople, the western bank of the Bosphorus, of the Sea of Marmara and of the Dardanelles, as well as southern Thrace to the Enos-Midia line, should not henceforth be incorporated into the Russian Empire.

Similarly, and by strategic necessity, that part of the Asiatic shore that lies between the Bosphorus, the river Sakharia and a point to be determined on the Gulf of Ismid, and the islands of the Sea of Marmara, the islands of Imbros and Tenedos, must be incorporated into the [Russian] Empire.

The special interests of France and of Great Britain in the region designated above will be scrupulously respected.

The Imperial Government entertains the hope that the above considerations will be sympathetically received by the two allied Governments. The said allied Governments are assured similar understanding on the part of the Imperial Government for the realization of plans which they may form in other regions of the Ottoman Empire or elsewhere.

(b) *British* Aide-Mémoire *to the Russian Government, 12 March 1915*
Subject to the war being carried on and brought to a successful conclusion, and to the desiderata of Great Britain and France in the Ottoman Empire and elsewhere being realized, as indicated in the Russian communication herein referred to, His Majesty's Government will agree to the Russian Government's *aide-mémoire* relative to Constantinople and the Straits, the text of which was communicated to His Britannic Majesty's Ambassador by his Excellency M. Sazonof on 4 March instant.

(c) *British Memorandum to the Russian Government, 12 March 1915*

... From the British *aide-mémoire* it follows that the desiderata of His Majesty's Government, however important they may be to British interests in other parts of the world, will contain no condition which could impair Russia's control over the territories described in the Russian *aide-mémoire* of 4 March, 1915.

In view of the fact that Constantinople will always remain a trade *entrepôt* for South-Eastern Europe and Asia Minor, His Majesty's Government will ask that Russia shall, when she comes into possession of it, arrange for a free port for goods in transit to and from non-Russian territory. His Majesty's Government will also ask that there shall be commercial freedom for merchant-ships passing through the Straits, as M. Sazonof has already promised. ...

Sir E. Grey points out that it will obviously be necessary to take into consideration the whole question of the future interests of France and Great Britain in what is now Asiatic Turkey; and, in formulating the desiderata of His Majesty's Government with regard to the Ottoman Empire, he must consult the French as well as the Russian Government. As soon, however, as it becomes known that Russia is to have Constantinople at the conclusion of the war, Sir E. Grey will wish to state that throughout the negotiations, His Majesty's Government have stipulated that the Mussulman Holy Places and Arabia shall under all circumstances remain under independent Mussulman dominion.

Sir E. Grey is as yet unable to make any definite proposal on any point of the British desiderata; but one of the points of the latter will be the revision of the Persian portion of the Anglo-Russian Agreement of 1907 so as to recognise the present neutral sphere as a British sphere ...

(d) Note Verbale *communicated by M. Paléologue to M. Sazonov, 18 April 1915*

The Government of the [French] Republic will give its agreement to the Russian *aide-mémoire* addressed by M. Isvolsky to M. Delcassé on 6 March last, relating to Constantinople and the Straits, on condition that war shall be prosecuted until victory and that France and Great Britain realise their plans in the East as elsewhere, as it is stated in the Russian *aide-mémoire*.

British Documents on Foreign Policy, 1919–39, London, 1947 ff, 1st series, iv, pp. 635–8.

DOCUMENT 28   **THE BALFOUR DECLARATION,
2 NOVEMBER 1917**

The declaration was addressed to Dr Chaim Weizmann, the Zionist leader.

I have much pleasure in conveying to you, on behalf of his [sic] Majesty's
Government, the following declaration of sympathy with Jewish Zionist
aspirations which has been submitted to and approved by the Cabinet:

His Majesty's Government view with favour the establishment in
Palestine of a National Home for the Jewish People, and will use its best
endeavours to facilitate the achievement of this object, it being clearly
understood that nothing shall be done which may prejudice the civil and
religious rights of existing non-Jewish communities in Palestine, or the rights
and political status enjoyed by Jews in any other country.

H. W. V. Temperley (ed.), *A History of the Peace Conference of Paris*,
London, 1920–24, vi, p. 170.

DOCUMENT 29   **WOODROW WILSON'S FOURTEEN POINTS,
JANUARY 1918**

*The list of peace aims, known as the Fourteen Points, which President
Woodrow Wilson enunciated in January 1918, was broadly endorsed by the
Allies and accepted as the basis for an armistice by the Germans. Points XI
and XII referred to the Balkans and the Ottoman Empire.*

XI. Roumania, Serbia, and Montenegro should be evacuated; occupied
territories restored; Serbia accorded free and secure access to the sea; and
the relations of the several Balkan states to one another determined by
friendly counsel along historically established lines of allegiance and
nationality; and international guarantees of the political and economic
independence and territorial integrity of the several Balkan states should be
entered into.

XII. The Turkish portions of the present Ottoman Empire should be
assured a secure sovereignty, but the other nationalities which are now
under Turkish rule should be assured an undoubted security of life and an
absolutely unmolested opportunity of autonomous development, and the
Dardanelles should be permanently opened as a free passage to the ships
and commerce of all nations under international guarantees.

D. Lloyd George, *Memoirs of the Peace Conference*, Howard Fertig, New
York, 1972, i, pp. 37–8.

DOCUMENT 30   EMIR FAISAL'S MEMORANDUM TO THE
SUPREME COUNCIL AT THE PARIS PEACE
CONFERENCE, 1 JANUARY 1919

At the Paris Peace Conference, Faisal, the leader of the Hedjaz delegation,
endeavoured to speak on behalf of all the Arab peoples inhabiting Arabia
and the Fertile Crescent.

The country from a line Alexandretta–Persia southward to the Indian Ocean
is inhabited by 'Arabs' – by which we mean people of closely related Semitic
stocks, all speaking the one language, Arabic. The non-Arabic-speaking
elements in this area do not, I believe, exceed one per cent of the whole.

The aim of the Arab nationalist movements (of which my father became
the leader in war after combined appeals from the Syrian and Meso-
potamian branches) is to unite the Arabs eventually into one nation. As an
old member of the Syrian Committee I commanded the Syrian revolt, and
had under me Syrians, Mesopotamians, and Arabians.

We believe that our ideal of Arab unity in Asia is justified beyond need of
argument. If argument is required, we would point to the general principles
accepted by the Allies when the United States joined them, to our splendid
past, to the tenacity with which our race has for 600 years resisted Turkish
attempts to absorb us, and, in a lesser degree, to what we tried our best to
do in this war as one of the Allies.

My father has a privileged place among Arabs, as their successful leader,
and as the head of their greatest family, and as Sherif of Mecca. He is
convinced of the ultimate triumph of the ideal of unity, if no attempt is
made now to force it, by imposing an artificial political unity on the whole,
or to hinder it, by dividing the area as spoils of war among great Powers.

The unity of the Arabs in Asia has been made more easy of late years,
since the development of railways, telegraphs, and air-roads. In old days the
area was too huge, and in parts necessarily too thinly peopled, to
communicate common ideas readily.

The various provinces of Arab Asia – Syria, Irak, Jezireh, Hedjaz, Nejd,
Yemen – are very different economically and socially, and it is impossible to
constrain them into one frame of government.

We believe that Syria, an agricultural and industrial area thickly peopled
with sedentary classes, is sufficiently advanced politically to manage her
own internal affairs. We feel also that foreign technical advice and help will
be a most valuable factor in our national growth. We are willing to pay for
this help in cash: we cannot sacrifice for it any part of the freedom we have
just won for ourselves by force of arms.

Jezireh and Irak are two huge provinces, made up of three civilised towns,
divided by large wastes thinly peopled by semi-nomadic tribes. The world
wishes to exploit Mesopotamia rapidly, and we therefore believe that the
system of government there will have to be buttressed by the men and
material resources of a great foreign Power. We ask, however, that the

Government be Arab in principle and spirit, the selective rather than the elective principle being necessarily followed in the neglected districts, until time makes the broader basis possible. The main duty of the Arab Government there would be to oversee the educational processes which are to advance the tribes to the moral level of the towns.

The Hedjaz is mainly a tribal area, and the government will remain, as in the past, suited to patriarchal conditions. We appreciate these better than Europe, and propose therefore to retain our complete independence there.

The Yemen and Nejd are not likely to submit their cases to the Peace Conference. They look after themselves, and adjust their own relations with the Hedjaz and elsewhere.

In Palestine the enormous majority of the people are Arabs. The Jews are very close to the Arabs in blood, and there is no conflict of character between the two races. In principles we are absolutely at one. Nevertheless, the Arabs cannot risk assuming the responsibility of holding level the scales in the clash of races and religions that have, in this one province, so often involved the world in difficulties. They would wish for the effective super-position of a great trustee, so long as a representative local administration commended itself by actively promoting the material prosperity of the country.

Hurewitz, [51], pp.38–9.

DOCUMENT 31   **LORD CURZON, THE BRITISH FOREIGN SECRETARY, ON THE FUTURE OF CONSTANTINOPLE, 1919**

In January 1919, following an animated discussion of the question in the Eastern Committee, Curzon summarised the arguments for and against the expulsion of the Turks from Constantinople.

It was pointed out that the expulsion of the Turk from Constantinople was one of the avowed objects of the war. Great Britain and France agreed in 1915 to hand it over – together with the Straits and a considerable strip of land on both the European and Asiatic shores – to Russia, as the prize of victory in the conflict. At a later date, in the Statement of the War Aims of the Allies, promulgated in reply to President Wilson in January 1917, the ejection of the Turk from Europe was explicitly included.

The language of President Wilson pointed to a similar conclusion. Neither the Turk nor anyone else could therefore have any ground for surprise if the threat were now carried out. It has been made known both to him and to the entire Eastern world.

The arguments that were used in favour of its fulfilment were the following. For nearly five centuries the presence of the Turk in Europe has been a source of distraction, intrigue, and corruption in European politics, of oppression, and misrule to the subject nationalities, and an incentive to undue and overweening ambitions in the Moslem world. It has encouraged the Turk to regard himself as a Great Power, and has enabled him to impose upon others the same illusion. It has placed him in a position to play off one Power against another, and in their jealousies and his own machinations to find pretexts for his continued immunity. It has been an inexpugnable barrier to the solution of the Balkan problem or the full emancipation of the Balkan peoples. It has been an equal obstacle to the proper or good government of his own people, whose resources have been squandered in the polluted *coulisses* of Constantinople, or in the expenditure required for the upkeep of military and naval forces disproportionate to the real strength or requirements of the Turkish nation.

An opportunity of cutting out and getting rid for ever of this plague spot, such as has not arisen for centuries, has now presented itself. It may not recur for generations. The world is looking for great solutions. Let not this occasion, it was argued, be missed of purging the earth of one of its most pestilent roots of evil.

On the other hand it was urged that the disappearance of the Turk while removing an admitted ill, will introduce a number of new and unforeseen complications in its place; that if his claws be clipped, and all power of offence taken away, he will become an innocuous if not a positive respectable creature; that, once his friendly relations with ourselves are resumed, he may even provide a benevolent buffer between the ambitions of Europe and our own Eastern possessions; that his expulsion would be a grave outrage to Mohammedan sentiment throughout the world, and more particularly in India, where the successive blows under which the Sultan and his dominions have reeled in recent years are said to have created an unfavourable impression, and where this final sentence would be regarded as a cruel affront to Islam, prepared or connived in by Great Britain, the second greatest Mohammedan power in the world.

In reply, however, to these forebodings, it was pointed out by many who have direct knowledge of India that the Indian Mohammedans have never attached any particular sanctity or reverence to Constantinople; that they have grown accustomed to the gradual diminution of the Ottoman power in Europe and Africa; that they have borne without excitement his expulsion from the Holy Places in the present war; that they have even fought against the Turkish armies in more than one campaign; and that they evinced neither astonishment nor regret when the intentions of the Allies with regard to Constantinople were announced to the world. So far indeed from being surprised by their fulfilment, they would be more likely to regard it as a mark of Allied weakness or of the Sultan's diplomatic triumph if they were now abandoned. In this context it was remarked that the present attitude of the Turk at Constantinople, and his evasions and pretexts in respect of carrying out the armistice, are an eloquent confirmation of the position which he may be expected to assume should his adversaries be so weak or so foolish as to spare him.

Public Record Office, London, ADM 116/3239.

DOCUMENT 32   THE TURKISH NATIONAL PACT, 28 JANUARY 1920

In January 1920 the Ottoman Chamber of Deputies approved a list of principles, known as the National Pact, which had been drawn up for the most part by the Turkish Nationalists in Ankara.

The members of the Ottoman Chamber of Deputies recognise and affirm that the independence of the State and the future of the Nation can be assured by an absolute adherence to the following principles, which represent the maximum of sacrifices which can be endured to achieve a just and lasting peace, and that the continued existence of a stable Ottoman Sultanate and society is impossible if we do not adhere to the said principles:

Article 1. Inasmuch as it is necessary that the destinies of the portions of the Turkish Empire which are peopled by Arab majorities, and which on the conclusion of the Armistice of October 30, 1918, were under occupation by enemy forces, should be determined in accordance with a free plebiscite of the inhabitants, all such territories (whether within or outside the lines of the said Armistice) which are inhabited by an Ottoman Muslim majority, who are united in religion, in race and in aim, are imbued with sentiments of mutual regard, are prepared for individual sacrifice, and have an absolute respect for one another's racial rights and for social circumstances, form a whole which does not admit of division for any reason in truth or in law.

Article 2. We are willing that, in the case of the three *sancaks* which united themselves by ... a general vote to the mother country when they were first free, recourse would again be had, if necessary, to a free popular vote.

Article 3. The determination also of the juridical status of Western Thrace, which has been made dependent on the Turkish peace, must be effected in accordance with a vote which shall be given by the inhabitants, in complete freedom.

Article 4. The security of the city of Istanbul (which is the seat of the Kalifate of Islam, the capital of the Sultanate, and the headquarters of the Ottoman Government) and likewise the security of the Sea of Marmara must be protected from every danger. Provided this principle is maintained, whatever decision may be arrived at jointly by us and all other Governments concerned, regarding the opening of the Bosphorus to the commerce and traffic of the world, shall be valid.

Article 5. The rights of Minorities as defined in the treaties concluded between the Entente powers and their enemies and certain of their associates shall be confirmed and assured by us – in reliance on the belief that the Muslim minorities in neighbouring countries will also be given the benefit of the same rights.

Article 6. It is a fundamental condition of our life and continued existence that we, like every country, should enjoy complete independence and liberty in the matter of assuring the means of our development, in order that our national and economic development may be so rendered possible, that it should be possible to conduct our affairs in the form of a more modern and regular administration.

For this reason we are opposed to restriction inimical to our development in political, judicial, financial, and other fields.

The conditions of settlement of what our indebtedness shall be shown to be, shall likewise not be contrary to such principles.

Emin, [26], pp. 153–5.

DOCUMENT 33   A STATEMENT OF BRITISH POLICY ON
PALESTINE, 1922

Winston Churchill, the Colonial Secretary, coming under both Arab nationalist and Zionist pressure, endeavoured to clarify British policy regarding Palestine in a statement made public on 1 July 1922.

The Secretary of State for the Colonies has given renewed consideration to the existing political situation in Palestine, with a very earnest desire to arrive at a settlement of the outstanding questions which have given rise to uncertainty and unrest among certain sections of the population. After consultation with the High Commissioner for Palestine the following statement has been drawn up. It summarises the essential parts of the correspondence that has already taken place between the Secretary of State and a Delegation from the Moslem Christian Society of Palestine, which has been for some time in England, and it states the further conclusions which have since been reached.

The tension which has prevailed from time to time in Palestine is mainly due to apprehensions, which are entertained both by sections of the Arab and by sections of the Jewish population. These apprehensions, so far as the

Arabs are concerned, are partly based upon exaggerated interpretations of the meaning of the Declaration favouring the establishment of a Jewish National Home in Palestine, made on behalf of His Majesty's Government on 2nd November, 1917. Unauthorised statements have been made to the effect that the purpose in view is to create a wholly Jewish Palestine. Phrases have been used such as that Palestine is to become 'as Jewish as England is English'. His Majesty's Government regard any such expectation as impracticable and have no such aim in view. Nor have they at any time contemplated, as appears to be feared by the Arab Delegation, the disappearance or the subordination of the Arabic population, language or culture in Palestine. They would draw attention to the fact that the terms of the Declaration referred to do not contemplate that Palestine as a whole should be converted into a Jewish National Home, but that such a Home should be founded *in Palestine*. In this connection it has been observed with satisfaction that at the meeting of the Zionist Congress, the supreme governing body of the Zionist Organisation, held at Carlsbad in September, 1921, a resolution was passed expressing as the official statement of Zionist aims 'the determination of the Jewish people to live with the Arab people on terms of unity and mutual respect, and together with them to make the common home into a flourishing community, the upbuilding of which may assure to each of its peoples an undisturbed development.'

It is also necessary to point out that the Zionist Commission in Palestine, now termed the Palestine Zionist Executive, has not desired to possess, and does not possess, any share in the general administration of the country. Nor does the special position assigned to the Zionist Organisation in Article IV of the Draft Mandate for Palestine imply any such functions. That special position relates to the measures to be taken in Palestine affecting the Jewish population, and contemplates that the Organisation may assist in the general development of the country, but does not entitle it to share in any degree in its Government.

Further, it is contemplated that the status of all citizens of Palestine in the eyes of the law shall be Palestinian, and it has never been intended that they, or any section of them, should possess any other juridical status.

So far as the Jewish population of Palestine are concerned, it appears that some among them are apprehensive that His Majesty's Government may depart from the policy embodied in the Declaration of 1917. It is necessary, therefore, once more to affirm that these fears are unfounded, and that that Declaration, reaffirmed by the Conference of the Principal Allied Powers at San Remo and again in the Treaty of Sèvres, is not susceptible of change. ...

Parliamentary Papers, 1922, Cmd. 1700, pp. 17–21.

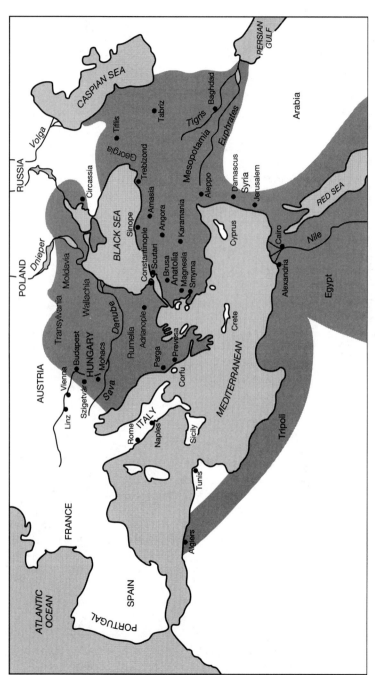

The Ottoman Empire under Suleiman

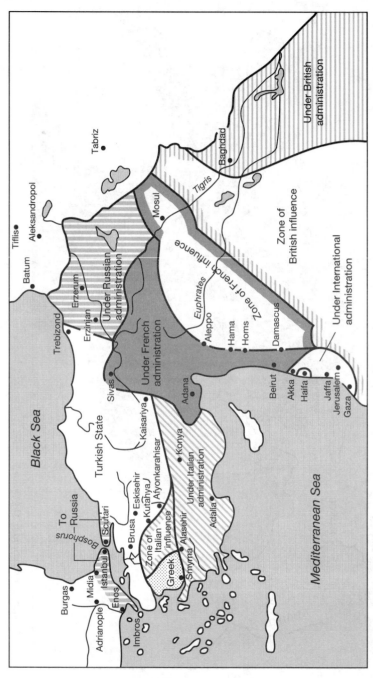

The partitioning of Turkey according to the secret agreements of 1915–17

BIBLIOGRAPHY

(The place of publication is London unless otherwise stated.)

1 Albrecht-Carrié, R., (ed.), *The Concert of Europe*, Macmillan, 1968.
2 Ancel, J., *Manuel Historique de la Question d'Orient*, Delagrave, Paris, 1923.
3 Anderson, M. S., *The Eastern Question, 1774–1923*, Macmillan, 1966.
4 Anderson, M. S., *The Great Powers and the Near East, 1774–1923*, Edward Arnold, 1970.
5 Antonius, G., *The Arab Awakening*, Hamilton, 1938.
6 Bailey, F. E., *British Policy and the Turkish Reform Movement*, Harvard University Press, Cambridge, Mass., 1942.
7 Blaisdell, D. C., *European Financial Control in the Ottoman Empire*, Columbia University Press, New York, 1929.
8 Bolsover, G. H., 'Nicholas I and the Partition of Turkey', *Slavonic and East European Review*, xxvii, 1948–49.
9 Cecil, G., *Life of Robert, Marquis of Salisbury*, Hodder and Stoughton, 1921.
10 Chamberlain, M. E., *British Foreign Policy in the Age of Palmerston*, Longman, 1980.
11 Choublier, M., *La Question d'Orient avant le Traité de Berlin*, Arthur Rousseau, Paris, 1899.
12 Churchill, W. S., *The World Crisis: the Aftermath*, Thornton and Butterworth, 1923–31.
13 Clayton, D. G., *Britain and the Eastern Question*, Lion Library, 1970.
14 Crawley, C. W., *The Question of Greek Independence, 1821–1833*, Cambridge University Press, 1930.
15 Dakin, D., *The Greek Struggle in Macedonia, 1897–1913*, Institute for Balkan Studies, Thessaloniki, 1966.
16 Dakin, D., *The Unification of Greece, 1770–1923*, Benn, 1972.
17 Dakin, D., *The Greek Struggle for Independence*, Batsford, 1973.
18 Davison, R. H., *Reform in the Ottoman Empire, 1856–1876*, Princeton University Press, 1963.
19 Davison, R. H., *Turkey*, Eothen Press, 1981.
20 Devereux, R. *The First Ottoman Constitutional Period*, Johns Hopkins University Press, Baltimore, 1963.

21   Dodwell, H. H., *The Founder of Modern Egypt*, Cambridge University Press, 1931.
22   Driault, E., *La Question d'Orient*, Felix Alcan, Paris, 1909.
23   Dyer, G. 'The Turkish Armistice of 1918', *Middle Eastern Studies*, viii, 1972.
24   Earle, E. M., *Turkey, The Great Powers and the Baghdad Railway*, Macmillan, New York, 1923.
25   East, W. G., *The Union of Moldavia and Wallachia, 1859*, Cambridge University Press, 1929.
26   Emin, A., *Turkey in the World War*, Yale University Press, New Haven, 1930.
27   Evans, L., *United States Policy and the Partition of Turkey, 1914–24*, Johns Hopkins University Press, Baltimore, 1965.
28   Florinsky, M. T., *Russia*, Macmillan, New York, 1967.
29   Foreign Office handbook, *History of the Eastern Question*, H.M.S.O, 1918.
30   Friedman, I., 'The McMahon–Hussein Correspondence and the Question of Palestine', *Journal of Contemporary History*, v, 1970.
31   Gewehr, W. M., *The Rise of Nationalism in the Balkans*, Archon Books, 1967.
32   Gillard, D., *The Struggle for Asia, 1828–1914*, Methuen, 1977.
33   Gleason J. H., *The Genesis of Russophobia in Great Britain, 1815–41*, Harvard University Press, Cambridge, Mass., 1950.
34   Gottlieb, W. W., *Studies in Secret Diplomacy*, Allen and Unwin, 1957.
35   Grenville, J. A. S., *Lord Salisbury and Foreign Policy*, Athlone Press, 1964.
36   Harris, D., *A Diplomatic History of the Balkan Crisis of 1875–1878: the First Year*, Stanford University Press, 1936.
37   Headlam-Morley, J. W., *Studies in Diplomatic History*, Methuen, 1930.
38   Helmreich, E. C., *The Diplomacy of the Balkan Wars, 1912–1913*, Harvard University Press, Cambridge, Mass., 1938.
39   Henderson, G. B., *Crimean War Diplomacy and other Historical Essays*, Jackson, Glasgow, 1947.
40   Henderson, G. B., 'German Economic Penetration of the Near East, 1870–1914', *Economic History Review*, xviii, 1948.
41   Higgins, T., *Winston Churchill and the Dardanelles*, Heinemann, 1963.
42   Holland Rose, J., *Pitt and the Great War*, Bell, 1911.
43   Holland Rose, J., 'The Political Reactions of Bonaparte's Eastern Expedition', *English Historical Review*, xliv, 1929.
44   Holt, P. M., *Egypt and the Fertile Crescent 1516–1922*, Longman, 1966.
45   Holt, P. M., Lampton, K. S. and Lewis, B. (eds), *The Cambridge History of Islam*, i, *The Central Islamic Lands*, Cambridge University Press, 1970.

46   Hornik, M. P., 'The Mission of Sir Henry Drummond Wolff to Constantinople, 1885–7', *English Historical Review*, lv, 1940.
47   Hoskins, H. L., *British Routes to India*, Frank Cass, 1928.
48   Hourani, A., *Europe and the Middle East*, University of California Press, Berkeley, 1986.
49   Howard, H. N., *The Partition of Turkey 1913–1923*, University of Oklahoma Press, Norman, 1931.
50   Howard, H. N., *The King–Crane Commission*, Constable, 1963.
51   Hurewitz, J. C., *Diplomacy in the Near and Middle East*, D. van Nostrand, Princeton, 1956.
52   Hyam, R., *Britain's Imperial Century, 1815–1914*, Batsford, 1976.
53   Inalcik, H., *The Ottoman Empire, 1300–1600*, Weidenfeld and Nicolson, 1973.
54   Jefferson, M. M., 'Lord Salisbury and the Eastern Question, 1890–1898', *Slavonic and East European Review*, xxxix, 1960–61.
55   Jelavich, B., *The Ottoman Empire, the Great Powers and the Straits Question, 1870–1887*, Indiana University Press, Bloomington, 1973.
56   Jelavich, B., *St. Petersburg and Moscow: Tsarist and Soviet Foreign Policy, 1814–1974*, Indiana University Press, Bloomington, 1974.
57   Jelavich, B., *History of the Balkans*, Cambridge University Press, 1983.
58   Kann, R., *A History of the Habsburg Empire, 1526–1918*, University of California Press, Berkeley, 1974.
59   Kedourie, E., *England and the Middle East*, Bowes & Bowes, 1956.
60   Kelly, J. B., *Britain and the Persian Gulf 1795–1880*, Clarendon Press, Oxford, 1963.
61   Kent, M., *The Great Powers and the End of the Ottoman Empire*, George Allen and Unwin, 1984.
62   Kinross, Lord, *Atatürk: The Rebirth of a Nation*, Weidenfeld and Nicolson, 1964.
63   Kirk, G. E., *A Short History of the Middle East*, Methuen, 1964.
64   Klieman, A. S., 'Britain's War Aims in the Middle East in 1915', *Journal of Contemporary History*, iii, 1968.
65   Laffin, J., *Damn the Dardanelles*, Osprey, 1980.
66   Landes, D. S., *Bankers and Pashas*, Heinemann, 1958.
67   Lewis, B., *The Emergence of Modern Turkey*, Oxford University Press, 1961.
68   Lloyd George, D., *The Truth about the Peace Treaties*, Gollancz, 1938.
69   Longrigg, S. H., *Syria and Lebanon under French Mandate*, Oxford University Press, 1958.
70   Longrigg, S. H., *Iraq, 1900–1950*, Oxford University Press, 1953.
71   Macfie, A. L., 'The British Decision regarding the Future of Constantinople, 1918–21', *The Historical Journal*, xviii, 1975.
72   Macfie, A. L., 'The Straits Question: The Conference of Lausanne, November 1922–July 1923', *Middle Eastern Studies*, xv, 1979.

73   Macfie, A. L., 'The Chanak Affair', *Balkan Studies*, xx, 1979.
74   Macfie, A. L., 'The Straits Question in the First World War, 1914–18', *Middle Eastern Studies*, xix, 1983.
75   Macfie, A. L., *Atatürk*, Longman, 1994.
76   Mardin, S., *The Genesis of Young Ottoman Thought*, Princeton University Press, 1962.
77   Marlowe, J., *Anglo-Egyptian Relations, 1800–1953*, Cresset, 1954.
78   Marlowe, J., *The Making of the Suez Canal*, Cresset, 1964.
79   Marriott, J. A. R., *The Eastern Question*, Clarendon Press, Oxford, 1918.
80   Medlicott, W. N., *The Congress of Berlin and After*, Methuen, 1938.
81   Miller, W., *The Ottoman Empire and its Successors, 1801–1927*, Cambridge University Press, 1934.
82   Millman, R., *Britain and the Eastern Question, 1875–1878*, Clarendon Press, Oxford, 1979.
83   Monroe, E., *Britain's Moment in the Middle East, 1914–1956*, Methuen, 1965.
84   Monypenny, W. F. and Buckle, G. E., *The Life of Benjamin Disraeli*, John Murray, 1920.
85   Mosely, P. E., *Russian Diplomacy and the Opening of the Eastern Question in 1838 and 1839*, Russell and Russell, New York, 1934.
86   Mosse, W. E., *The Rise and Fall of the Crimean System, 1855–1871*, Macmillan, 1963.
87   Nicolson, H., *Curzon: the Last Phase, 1919–1925*, Constable, 1937.
88   Nicolson, H., *The Congress of Vienna, 1812–1822*, Methuen, 1961.
89   Platt, D. C. M., *Finance, Trade and Politics in British Foreign Policy, 1815–1914*, Oxford University Press, 1968.
90   Puryear, V. J., *England, Russia and the Straits Question, 1844–1856*, University of California Press, Berkeley, 1931.
91   Puryear, V. J., *International Economics and Diplomacy in the Near East, 1834–1853*, Stanford University Press, 1935.
92   Puryear, V. J., *Napoleon and the Dardanelles*, University of California Press, Berkeley, 1951.
93   Ramsaur, E., *The Young Turks*, Princeton University Press, New Jersey, 1957.
94   Robinson, R. and Gallagher, J., *Africa and the Victorians*, Macmillan, 1961.
95   Roider, K. A., *Austria's Eastern Question*, Princeton University Press, New Jersey, 1982.
96   Ryan, A., *The Last of the Dragomans*, Bles, 1951.
97   Sacher, H. M., *The Emergence of the Middle East, 1914–1924*, Allen Lane, 1969.
98   Searight, S., *The British and the Middle East*, East-West Publications, 1979.
99   Seton-Watson, R. W., *Disraeli, Gladstone and the Eastern Question*, Frank Cass, 1933.

100 Seton-Watson, R. W., *A History of the Rumanians*, Cambridge University Press, 1934.

101 Sorel, A., *The Eastern Question in the Eighteenth Century*, New York, 1969.

102 Stavrianos, L. S., *The Balkans since 1453*, Rinehart, New York, 1958.

103 Stavrianos, L. S., *The Balkans, 1815–1914*, Holt, Rinehart and Winston, New York, 1963.

104 Stein, L., *The Balfour Declaration*, Vallentine Mitchell, 1961.

105 Sumner, B. H., *Russia and the Balkans, 1870–1880*, Oxford University Press, 1937.

106 Sykes, C., *Cross Roads to Israel*, Collins, 1965.

107 Taylor, A. J. P., *The Habsburg Monarchy, 1809–1918*, Harper Torchbooks, New York, 1948.

108 Taylor, A. J. P., *The Struggle for Mastery in Europe*, Clarendon Press, Oxford, 1954.

109 Temperley, H. W. V., 'The Treaty of Paris of 1856 and its Execution', *Journal of Modern History*, iv, 1932.

110 Temperley, H. W. V., *England and the Near East: The Crimea*, Archon Books, Hamden, Conn., 1964.

111 Temperley, H. W. V., *The Foreign Policy of Canning 1822–1827*, Cass, 1966.

112 Temperley, H. W. V., *History of Serbia*, Fertig, New York, 1969.

113 Thomson, D., *Europe since Napoleon*, Penguin Books, 1971.

114 Trumpener, U., *Germany and the Ottoman Empire*, Princeton University Press, 1968.

115 Ubicini, M. A., *La Question d'Orient devant l'Europe*, Dentu, Paris, 1854.

116 Weber, F. G., *Eagles and the Crescent*, Cornell University Press, Ithaca, 1970.

117 Webster, C. K., *The Foreign Policy of Palmerston, 1830–1941*, Bell, 1951.

118 Wolf, J., *The Diplomatic History of the Baghdad Railroad*, University of Missouri, 1936.

119 Woodhouse, C. M., *The Greek War of Independence*, Hutchinson, 1952.

120 Woodhouse, C. M., *The Battle of Navarino*, Hodder and Stoughton, 1965.

121 Wright, D. G., *Napoleon and Europe*, Longman, 1984.

122 Yapp, M.E., *The Making of the Modern Near East*, Longman, 1987

123 Zeine, Z. N., *The Struggle for Arab Independence*, Caravan Books, New York, 1960.

INDEX

The index includes principal persons and places mentioned, together with treaties, conventions, congresses and memoranda relating to the Eastern Question, as well as battles and wars.